The Invasion of Virginia 1781

Journal of the American Revolution Books highlight the latest research on new or lesser-known topics of the revolutionary era. The *Journal of the American Revolution* is an online resource and annual volume that provides educational, peer-reviewed articles by professional historians and experts in American Revolution studies, and is edited and managed by Todd Andrlik and Don N. Hagist.

Other Titles in the Series

The Burning of His Majesty's Schooner Gaspee:
An Attack on Crown Rule Before the American Revolution
by Steven Park

Grand Forage 1778: The Battleground Around New York City
by Todd W. Braisted

*The Road to Concord: How Four Stolen Cannon Ignited
the Revolutionary War*
by J. L. Bell

A JOURNAL OF THE AMERICAN REVOLUTION BOOK

THE
INVASION
OF
VIRGINIA
1781

MICHAEL CECERE

WESTHOLME
Yardley

Westholme Publishing, LLC
904 Edgewood Road
Yardley, Pennsylvania 19067
Visit our Web site at www.westholmepublishing.com

ISBN: 978-1-59416-279-4

Printed in the United States of America.

CONTENTS

Maps

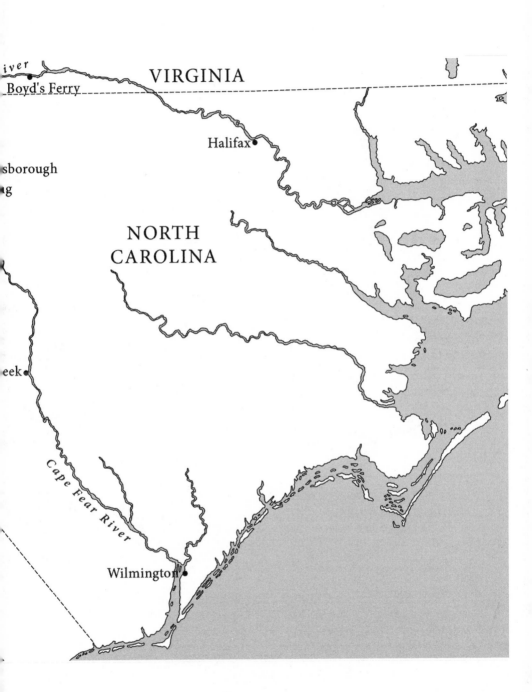

PR

KING GEORG

Rapidan River

Fredericksburg

North Anna River

Charlottesville

Rivanna River

South Anna River

Point of Fork

GOOCHLAND

James River

W

Appomattox River

VIRGINIA

PRINCE

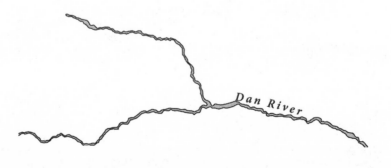

Dan River

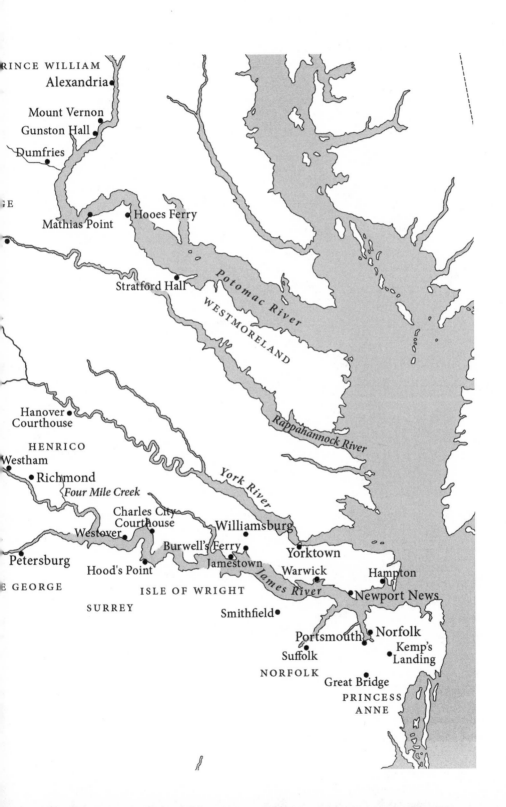

RINCE WILLIAM
Alexandria

Mount Vernon
Gunston Hall

Dumfries

GE

Mathias Point   Hooes Ferry

Stratford Hall

Potomac River

WESTMORELAND

Rappahannock River

Hanover
Courthouse

HENRICO

Westham

Richmond
Four Mile Creek

York River

Charles City
Courthouse
Westover   Williamsburg

Burwell's Ferry   Yorktown

Petersburg   Jamestown   Warwick

Hood's Point   Hampton

E GEORGE   ISLE OF WRIGHT   *James River*

                                     Newport News
SURREY

                    Smithfield

                         Portsmouth   Norfolk

                         Suffolk   Kemp's
                                        Landing
NORFOLK

                    Great Bridge
                    PRINCESS
                    ANNE

INTRODUCTION

N EARLY ALL OF THE ORIGINAL THIRTEEN AMERICAN COLONIES felt the sting of war and bloodshed within their borders during the American War for Independence. New Jersey proudly claims to be the crossroads of the Revolution with the Battles of Trenton, Princeton, and Monmouth. South Carolina claims to have endured the most engagements, with Charleston, Camden, Kings Mountain, and Cowpens, to name a few. New York has pride of place with Saratoga, recognized by many as the turning point of the war, and Massachusetts has the distinction of being the place where America's War for Independence started: at Lexington and Concord.

Surprisingly, Virginia, the largest of the original thirteen colonies (and affectionately known as the Old Dominion for its loyalty to the English monarchy during the English Civil War), saw relatively little fighting for the first six years of the Revolutionary War. While skirmishes at Hampton and Kemp's Landing in 1775 drew blood on both sides, and larger engagements at Great Bridge in December 1775 and Gwynn's Island in July 1776 resulted in significant military defeats for Virginia's royal governor, John Murray, the Earl of Dunmore, these engagements were small compared to the battles that occurred outside Virginia. Thus, although thousands of Virginians served on distant battlefields both north and south of the Old Dominion, Virginia was spared much of the bloodshed and destruction of the Revolutionary War within its own borders.

This changed in 1781 when British and American forces converged on the Old Dominion. The war's arrival in Virginia did not result from one particular decision or event but rather from a series of incidents and battles (beginning in the fall of 1780) that unfolded over a ten-month period, concluding with a monumental confrontation at Yorktown, Virginia, in October 1781. The outcome of this confrontation at Yorktown largely brought the Revolutionary War to its victorious end for America.

The events that led to this pivotal battle in southeastern Virginia are the focus of this book.

One

"To Make a Solid Move into North Carolina"

FALL 1780

G ENERAL HENRY CLINTON, THE RANKING COMMANDER OF British forces in America in 1780, received the news from South Carolina with much satisfaction. Lord Charles Cornwallis, with a force of approximately two thousand British troops, had routed a larger American army under General Horatio Gates outside of Camden, South Carolina, in mid-August. Cornwallis's success at Camden was the latest in a string of British victories in South Carolina that had begun three months earlier in May, when the American Southern army under General Benjamin Lincoln surrendered to General Clinton himself at Charleston, South Carolina. Clinton had returned to New York, which was Britain's principle post in America, in June, satisfied that his strategy to shift the bulk of British offensive operations to the southern colonies was working. The news of Cornwallis's victory at Camden seemed to confirm this.

When General Clinton returned to New York, he did so confident that the British force that remained in South Carolina under General

Cornwallis, some 4,200 troops, was sufficient to maintain British control there.[1] Clinton stressed to Cornwallis that maintaining British control of the newly won province should be his top priority:

> I requested His Lordship [Cornwallis] would constantly regard the safety of Charleston and tranquility of South Carolina as the principal and indispensable objects of his attention. When the necessary arrangements for this purpose were completed, and the season suitable to operation in that climate should return, I left His Lordship at liberty, if he judged proper, to make a solid move into North Carolina, upon condition it could at the time be made without risking the safety of the posts committed to his charge [South Carolina].[2]

In other words, Cornwallis had Clinton's permission to subdue North Carolina once he was ready to do so, provided that such a move did not risk British control of Charleston or the rest of South Carolina.

Over the summer of 1780, Cornwallis strengthened British control of South Carolina, establishing a semicircle of strong outposts in the backcountry at Ninety-Six, Camden, and Georgetown to secure the middle of the colony and screen Charleston. Numerous smaller outposts were also established to protect British supply and communication lines between Charleston and these posts. Cornwallis's victory at Camden in August convinced him that it was time to march into North Carolina to energize the large number of loyalists who were reportedly there but afraid to show their support for Britain. Cornwallis believed that strong Tory support in North Carolina would allow him to easily subdue the rebellious province. Unfortunately for the British commander, rampant illness among his troops, exacerbated by the hot South Carolina summer, and unexpectedly strong resistance from rebel militia (led largely by General Thomas Sumter and Colonel Francis Marion), delayed his movement into North Carolina until the latter half of September. By the end of that month, however, Cornwallis's advance guard, led by Lieutenant Colonel Banastre Tarleton, crossed into North Carolina and entered Charlotte, then just a small town east of the Catawba River, against light opposition from local militia.[3]

Two weeks before Cornwallis commenced his march northward, he sent Major Patrick Ferguson, an experienced British officer, with hundreds of Tory militia and a detachment of New York and New Jersey provincial troops (regular troops raised in America for the duration of the war), into the western foothills of North Carolina to suppress rebel activity and screen the left flank of his army. Major Ferguson encamped at Gilbert Town in North Carolina in mid-September, about seventy miles west of Charlotte, and recruited hundreds of additional Tories to his force. He also issued a stern threat to all rebels, particularly those in the backcountry, declaring that, "If they did not desist from their opposition to the British arms, he would march his army over the mountains, hang their leaders, and lay their country waste with fire and sword."[4]

Instead of intimidating the frontiersmen into submission, however, Ferguson provoked them. His threat spread quickly throughout the frontier, and by the end of September hundreds of riflemen had assembled, eager to confront him. While the rebel riflemen gathered on the other side of the mountains, Major Ferguson remained in the vicinity of Gilbert Town, initially unaware of the growing danger and hoping to intercept a party of militia under Elijah Clarke of Georgia, a longtime nemesis of Ferguson and the British. Ferguson failed to find Clarke, and abandoned his search in late September when he discovered that over a thousand rebel riflemen were marching toward him from the mountains. He headed east in the direction of Charlotte and the support of Cornwallis. When he reached the Broad River in South Carolina, Ferguson appealed for assistance from local loyalists:

> Gentlemen:—Unless you wish to be eat up by an inundation of barbarians, who have begun by murdering an unarmed son before their aged father, and afterwards lopped off his arms, and who by their shocking cruelties and irregularities, give the best proof of their cowardice and want of discipline; I say, if you wish to be pinioned, robbed, and murdered, and see your wives and daughters, in four days, abused by the dregs of mankind—in short, if you wish or deserve to live, and bear the name of men, grasp your arms in a moment and run to camp.[5]

The tone of the letter conveyed Ferguson's disdain for the rifle-men, yet a message to Cornwallis a few days later, dated October 6, hinted at his concern:

My Lord: [The riflemen have] become an object of some con-sequence. Happily their leaders are obliged to feed their fol-lowers with such hopes, and so to flatter them with accounts of our weakness and fear, that, if necessary, I should hope for success against them myself; but numbers compared, that must be doubtful. I am on my march towards you. . . . Three or four hundred good soldiers, part dragoons, would finish the busi-ness. Something must be done soon. This is their last push in this quarter.[6]

Soon after Ferguson sent this message he decided to halt his flight, encamp at Kings Mountain, and await assistance from Cornwallis.

MAJOR PATRICK FERGUSON had approximately one thousand loyalist militia from the Carolinas under his command, of which two hun-dred were away from Kings Mountain foraging for supplies on Oc-tober 6. The provincial troops from New Jersey and New York only numbered about one hundred, but they were well trained and equal in ability to most British regulars.[7]

Ferguson placed his men on a steep ridge approximately sixty feet high and six hundred yards long. It varied in width from sixty to two hundred yards and was shaped like a foot, with the narrow portion, or heel, running southwest of the wider portion, or toes. There was little cover on the crest, as it was largely devoid of trees or brush. The sides of the hill and the surrounding area were wooded, however, and provided cover for anyone attempting to ascend the hill.

By October 6, approximately nine hundred mounted riflemen from the backwoods of Virginia and the Carolinas had assembled at Cowpens, South Carolina, about thirty miles west of Kings Moun-tain. Colonel William Campbell of Virginia had led two hundred Vir-ginians and joined riflemen from South Carolina under Colonels Thomas Brandon, William Hill, and Edward Lacy. Hundreds of

North Carolina riflemen under Colonels Isaac Shelby, John Sevier, Benjamin Cleveland, and Joseph McDowell were also there.[8] The officers met and selected Campbell to command, then headed east, riding through much of the night in the rain.

They reached Kings Mountain in the afternoon of October 7, tired, wet, and hungry, but eager to fight.

> When the patriots came near the mountain they halted, tied all their loose baggage to their saddles, fastened their horses, and left them under charge of a few men, and then prepared for an immediate attack [Colonel Isaac Shelby recalled]. About three o'clock the patriot force was led to the attack in four columns—Col. Campbell commanded the right center column, Col. Shelby the left center, Col. Sevier the right flank column, and Col. Cleveland the left flank. As they came to the foot of the mountain the right center and right flank columns deployed to the right, and the left center and left flank columns to the left.[9]

Colonel William Campbell described the initial phase of the battle:

> Col. Shelby's regiment and mine began the attack, and sustained the whole fire of the enemy for about ten minutes, while the other troops were forming around the height upon which the enemy were posted. The firing then became general, and as heavy as you can conceive for the number of men. The advantageous situation of the enemy, being the top of a steep ridge, obliged us to expose ourselves exceedingly; and the dislodging of them was almost equal to driving men from strong breastworks.[10]

Campbell urged his men forward, shouting, "Here they are, my brave boys, shout like hell, and fight like devils!"[11] The Virginians scurried up the steep slope using trees and boulders for cover. As they approached the crest, Major Ferguson ordered a bayonet charge to push them back. The Virginians, lacking bayonets, fled down the hill, where Campbell rallied them. The Tories returned to the crest and turned their attention to Colonel Shelby's North Carolinians. Shelby's men were opposite Campbell's, and were about to reach the crest when they too were pushed back by a bayonet charge. Shelby recalled years later that "as [the riflemen] would approach the summit, Ferguson would order a charge with fixed bayonet, which was always successful, for the riflemen retreated before the charging column slowly, still firing as they retired."[12]

The fight intensified as the rest of the riflemen joined the battle. James Collins, an American rifleman from South Carolina, recalled,

> We were soon in motion, every man throwing four or five balls in his mouth to prevent thirst, also to be in readiness to reload quick. The shot of the enemy soon began to pass over us like hail . . . We soon attempted to climb the hill, but were fiercely charged upon and forced to fall back to our first position; we tried a second time, but met the same fate; the fight seemed to become more furious.[13]

John Henry of North Carolina fell victim to one of Ferguson's bayonet charges. "We . . . advanced up the hill close to the Tory lines," he remembered.

> There was a log across a hollow that I took my stand by, and stepping one step back, I was safe from the British fire. I there remained firing until the British charged bayonet. When they made the charge they first fired their guns . . . I was preparing to fire when one of the advancing British . . . gave me a thrust through my hand and into my thigh.[14]

Ferguson's men chased Henry's comrades to the bottom of the hill and then returned to the crest to repeat the process. Time and again, Ferguson's troops forced the riflemen back, but only temporarily. Most of the frontiersmen rallied to their officers at the base of the hill and resumed the attack.

The entire hill was ablaze with gunfire and shrouded with smoke as the riflemen converged on the crest. Communication and coordination was difficult for both sides, but especially for the Americans, who were spread out. Many overcame this by following the pre-battle advice of Colonel Benjamin Cleveland: "Every man must consider himself an officer, and act from his own judgment. Fire as quick as you can, and stand your ground as long as you can. When you can do no better, get behind trees, or retreat; but I beg you not quite to run off. If we are repulsed, let us make a point of returning, and renewing the fight."[15] Largely on their own initiative, the riflemen maintained constant pressure on Ferguson's troops. Thomas Young recalled, "Ben Hollingsworth and myself took right up the side of the mountain, and fought from tree to tree . . . to the summit. I recollect I stood behind one tree and fired until the bark was nearly knocked off, and my eyes pretty well filled with it."[16]

Ferguson's situation grew increasingly desperate as riflemen began to reach the crest of the hill. Alexander Chesney, a local Tory fighting with Ferguson, noted that "the Americans who had been repulsed had regained their former stations and sheltered behind trees poured in an irregular destructive fire; in this manner the engagement was maintained near an hour, the mountaniers flying whenever there was danger of being charged by the Bayonet, and returning again so soon as the British detachment had faced about to repel another of their parties."[17]

Ferguson's reliance on the bayonet, coupled with the riflemen's deadly fire upon his exposed men, meant that the Tories suffered heavy casualties. A few Tories attempted to surrender, which provoked an angry response from Major Ferguson. One observer heard him exclaim that "he never would yield to such damned banditti."[18] Shortly after he made this statement, Ferguson was dead, shot from his horse by a number of riflemen. Command of the Tories fell to Captain Abraham DePeyser, who quickly surrendered. Sadly, a number of the riflemen were slow to give quarter, and many unfortunate Tories fell at the hands of the enraged riflemen while they attempted to surrender.

The Battle of Kings Mountain was a significant victory for the Americans. An important detachment of Cornwallis's army was virtually destroyed, and—as it consisted mostly of Tory militia—their loss dampened Tory enthusiasm to support Cornwallis's efforts in the Carolinas. Coming on the heels of major American defeats at

Charleston and Camden, the rebel victory at Kings Mountain boosted American morale in the South. It also caused Cornwallis to suspend his march into North Carolina until the situation in South Carolina stabilized. He left Charlotte and returned to South Carolina, where he established a strong post in Winnsboro, about thirty miles west of Camden. The return of British authority and rule in North Carolina would have to wait for the time being.

To ASSIST CORNWALLIS in subduing North Carolina, General Clinton had sent 2,200 troops under General Alexander Leslie from New York to Virginia in mid-October with instructions to "make a diversion in favor of Cornwallis, who by the time you arrive there will probably be acting in the back parts of North Carolina."[19] At the time he sent Leslie to Virginia, Clinton was unaware of Ferguson's defeat at Kings Mountain. He left it to General Leslie to determine how best to accomplish this diversion in support of Cornwallis, but suggested that Leslie "proceed up James River as high as possible, in order to seize or destroy any magazines the enemy may have at Petersburg, Richmond, or any of the places adjacent, and establish a post on the Elizabeth River."[20]

Intercepting much-needed supplies in Virginia that were destined for the remnants of the American Southern army in North Carolina would likely erode rebel resistance in North Carolina. Such resistance would further diminish if desperately needed Virginian reinforcements were detained in Virginia by Leslie's presence in the state. Both outcomes could hasten the fall of North Carolina to the British, but coordination between Cornwallis and Leslie was crucial for success, so Clinton instructed Leslie to establish communications with Cornwallis as soon as he arrived in Virginia.

General Leslie sailed for Virginia in mid-October, escorted by six British warships, the forty-gun *Romulus*, the thirty-two-gun *Blonde*, the sixteen-gun *Delight*, a twenty-gun privateer, and two row galleys.[21] Leslie's infantry force included troops from the Brigade of Guards, the Hessian Regiment von Bose, the Provincial King's American Regiment, a battalion of light infantry drawn from several provincial (American loyalist) corps in New York, a detachment of

German jaegers, a detachment of Seventeenth Light Dragoons, and some British and German artillerists.[22]

The expedition sailed into Chesapeake Bay on October 20, and Leslie immediately sent detachments ashore to gain intelligence and obtain pilots to navigate the local waters.[23] The following day, Leslie landed a detachment of cavalry and infantry at Portsmouth and two days later, on October 23, another detachment landed across the James River at Newport News, where they moved inland and, according to Thomas Jefferson, Virginia's governor, committed "horrid depredations."[24]

Leslie marched with this detachment and entered Hampton, where he learned through the local gazettes about Major Ferguson's stunning defeat in South Carolina just two weeks earlier. Leslie realized immediately that Cornwallis's movement into North Carolina would be hindered by Ferguson's defeat.[25] Anxious to receive word from Cornwallis on how to proceed (and unaware that Cornwallis had retreated back into South Carolina), Leslie concentrated his force at Portsmouth, which he fortified, and sent dispatches southward. He explained his actions to Clinton in New York, noting that a lack of river pilots for the James River, uncertainty about Lord Cornwallis's movements or wishes, and "the dissidence of the people of the country (who it was dangerous to leave behind us . . .) all led us to resolve unanimously that a post ought to be established at Portsmouth prior to our penetrating further into the country."[26] Realizing that Clinton would likely be disappointed in his decision not to proceed up the James River to raid rebel magazines and supply depots, Leslie added that "the country was acquainted with our destination some weeks before our arrival, which had given them time to take measures to oppose us by erecting batteries on the banks of the narrow parts of the James River, fortifying Richmond, and collecting a formidable militia."[27]

No such formidable militia or batteries awaited the British in Richmond or along the James River. Leslie had been misinformed.

Leslie's inactivity did not prevent Governor Thomas Jefferson from ordering the removal of over two thousand British and German prisoners of war from Charlottesville to Fort Frederick in western Maryland. These were the Convention prisoners from Saratoga, and they had just begun their fourth year of captivity. They had originally been held in Massachusetts, but in the winter of 1778–1779 Congress decided to move them south, and Charlottesville became their new residence. Virginia officials worried that the presence of Leslie's force in Portsmouth was a great temptation for many of the prisoners, so to prevent their escape (or rescue from Leslie), Jefferson arranged to send them to Fort Frederick in western Maryland. When it was discovered that the Maryland fort could not accommodate all of the prisoners, Jefferson decided to send only the eight hundred British captives, the assumption being that the 1,500 Hessians were less desirous of escaping to rejoin the war.[28]

While Jefferson arranged to secure the prisoners, he also grew more perplexed at the lack of activity by Leslie's force in Portsmouth. He speculated (somewhat accurately) to Samuel Huntington, president of the Continental Congress, that the enemy's "movements here had induced me to think they came in expectation of meeting with Lord Cornwallis in this country, that [Cornwallis's] precipitate retreat [from Charlotte] has left them without a concerted object, and that they were awaiting further orders."[29]

This was indeed at least partly the case. Leslie waited impatiently for word from Cornwallis and sent multiple dispatches southward, one of which was intercepted by the Virginians. Leslie's intercepted message confirmed to Virginia officials that his movements were in coordination with Cornwallis, or at least supposed to be, and that he was unsure how to proceed.

Leslie's uncertainty was finally resolved on November 9, when he received instructions from Cornwallis to abandon Portsmouth and sail to the Cape Fear River in North Carolina (and ultimately to Charleston to reinforce Cornwallis in South Carolina). Leslie took a few days to collect forage for his horses before he departed on November 15. He left behind in Portsmouth hundreds of runaway slaves who had risked their lives to escape to the British. Limited space on the ships caused Leslie to abandon the runaways in Portsmouth.

Two

Benedict Arnold
Invades Virginia

JANUARY 1781

I N NEW YORK, GENERAL CLINTON, DISAPPOINTED AT THE TURN OF events in the South, remained convinced that a British post near the mouth of the Chesapeake Bay was crucial for British success in the Carolinas. He explained in his memoirs that "my chief objects in sending expeditions to the Chesapeake were . . . to endeavor to destroy the stores collected at the head of James River for the supply of Gates's army, and to lay hold of some convenient post at its mouth for covering frigates—from whence we might obstruct the enemy's trade in those waters and, by commanding that noble river, prevent their forming depots on its banks for the service of Carolina."[1]

Within weeks of Leslie's departure from Virginia, Clinton resolved to send a second expedition there. Command of this 1,800-man force fell to the man who had transfered his allegiance, Brigadier General Benedict Arnold, a traitor to the American cause.

Rising above all other American officers in the first two years of the war for his bold deeds and accomplishments on the battlefield,

Benedict Arnold of Connecticut first attracted notice as the commander of a party of militia that marched into New York to capture Fort Ticonderoga on Lake Champlain in May 1775. Four months later, Colonel Arnold led a 1,100-man detachment of Continental troops on an epic march through the Maine and Canadian wilderness to strike Quebec. Although the attack on Quebec failed and Arnold was seriously wounded in the leg, he soon recovered and played a pivotal role in defending Lake Champlain. Promoted to brigadier general by Congress, Arnold's fleet of gunboats, constructed under his supervision over the summer of 1776, challenged a British invasion force from Canada in October 1776. Although Arnold's fleet was destroyed, its presence on Lake Champlain delayed the British timetable and forced them to cancel further operations on the lake until 1777.

In 1777, General Arnold once again emerged as one of America's greatest military heroes, boldly leading troops in the Battles of Saratoga in New York. Grievously wounded in the same leg that was injured at Quebec—a wound that affected him for the rest of his life—Arnold's leadership at Saratoga was instrumental in America's victory.

Arnold's wound prevented him from taking the field in 1778, and he instead found himself appointed military commander of Philadelphia after the British abandoned the city in June. It was during his tenure there that accusations of corruption surfaced— accusations that eventually led to a court-martial. Although Arnold only received a mild reprimand for his questionable conduct, he felt wronged by the tribunal. Arnold's long-held resentment of Congress over the issue of military rank now carried over to the army and contributed, along with simple greed, to his decision to betray the United States in 1780.

After an extended period of secret negotiations with the British, General Arnold agreed to help them capture the key American post of West Point, on the Hudson River. His transfer to that post in 1779 had placed Arnold, as commander, in the ideal position to hand the post over to the enemy without a fight. In late September 1780, Arnold delivered the defensive plans of West Point to a British officer: Major John André. André, who was dressed in civilian clothes, was subsequently apprehended by American militia on his way back to the British lines. The incriminating evidence on Major André exposed Arnold, who successfully fled to the British for his safety before he could be arrested. Although he had failed to deliver West Point to the British, the revelation of Arnold's betrayal was a tremendous blow to the American cause. One of America's best generals had turned on the country, and it was only natural to ask who else might be working for the British.

General Henry Clinton honored his terms with Arnold and made him a brigadier general in the British army. Expecting Arnold to do all he could to prove his worth to the British, and hoping that other American officers might follow Arnold's lead once they saw how generously he was treated, Clinton placed Arnold in command of the 1,800-man expedition to Virginia in December 1780.[2]

Clinton had two objectives for Arnold's expedition: to establish a secure British post in Portsmouth that would encourage loyalist Virginians in the counties of Princess Anne and Norfolk to step forward and support the British cause, and to disrupt the flow of supplies to the American Southern army in the Carolinas.[3] This meant that the British occupation of Portsmouth was not to be temporary; they were going to stay. General Arnold was given the latitude to strike at rebel supply depots throughout Virginia (and particularly up the James River), but only if such incursions did not threaten his hold on Portsmouth.

OVER TWENTY TRANSPORT SHIPS, escorted by the forty-four-gun *Charon*, the twenty-four-gun *Amphitrite*, the twenty-gun *Fowey*, the eighteen-gun *Hope*, and the sixteen-gun *Bonetta*, plus several smaller British warships and privateers, all under the command of Commodore Thomas Symonds, sailed out of New York harbor with General Arnold's troops on December 20, 1780, bound for Virginia.[4] Onboard the transports were over 750 soldiers from Lieutenant Colonel Thomas Dundas's 80th Edinburgh Royal Volunteers Regiment, a detachment of 110 German jaegers (riflemen) under Captain Johann Ewald, two loyalist American units, the Queen's Rangers with over 500 men, commanded by Lieutenant Colonel John Graves Simcoe of the British army, and the Loyal American Regiment, over

200 strong, commanded by Colonel Beverly Robinson Jr., a loyalist from New York who was also the nephew of a former disgraced Speaker of the Virginia House of Burgesses, John Robinson.[5] Arnold's newly formed American Legion, with only thirty American loyalists, a thirty-man detachment of pioneers, a forty-five-man company of loyalist New York riflemen under Captain John Althouse, and a seventy-man detachment of Royal Artillerists, completed the expedition.[6]

Hit by severe weather two days into the voyage, several transports with approximately four hundred troops were blown off course and failed to arrive off the Virginia capes with the rest of the fleet. Undeterred, Arnold pressed on into Chesapeake Bay and then westward into Hampton Roads.

Commodore James Barron, commander of the Virginia State Navy brig *Liberty*, spotted Arnold's fleet of nearly thirty vessels on December 30, as they entered Chesapeake Bay. Unsure of the fleet's origin or destination, Commodore Barron immediately sailed into Hampton to spread the alarm. Hampton merchant Jacob Wray rushed the news overland by dispatch rider to General Thomas Nelson, commander of the area's militia, in Yorktown. Nelson forwarded the news to Governor Thomas Jefferson in the capital (Richmond), who received it on the morning of December 31.

Unsure of the identity of the fleet and unwilling to muster the militia for a possible false alarm (the ships might have been French, after all), Jefferson waited for additional information, which he believed would soon follow, and passed Commodore Barron's report on to General Friedrich von Steuben, who was a few miles south of Richmond at Wilton Plantation. Steuben, a foreign volunteer from Prussia who was instrumental in developing a uniform system of military drill for the American army at Valley Forge during the winter of 1777–78, had arrived in Virginia in the fall of 1780 on his way to join the American Southern army in the Carolinas. Remaining in Virginia much longer than he intended, or desired, General Steuben was placed in the unenviable position of supervising the flow of reinforcements and supplies to the American Southern army in the Carolinas. As the highest-ranking Continental officer in Virginia, it was only natural for Governor Jefferson to turn to Steuben upon notice of the ships, informing him on December 31 that "I have this moment received information that 27 sail of vessels, 18 of which were square rigged, were yesterday morning just below Willoughby's point. No other circumstance being given to conjecture their force or destination, I am only able to dispatch Genl. Nelson into the lower country to take such measures as exigencies may require for the instant, until further information is received here. Then or in the meantime your aid and counsel will be deemed valuable."[7]

While Virginia's authorities struggled to determine the threat level of the mysterious ships, Arnold moved quickly to exploit the confusion caused by his sudden arrival.

Arnold's fleet anchored several miles up the James River, just off Newport News on the evening of December 30, and the next day he transferred his infantry onto smaller vessels (some of which had been captured from the Virginians the day before) in order to better navigate the broad, shallow James River. Securing pilots to help navigate the tricky river channel was a priority for Arnold, so on the evening of December 31 he sent a three-hundred-man detachment ashore to reconnoiter and obtain the necessary river pilots.[8]

Captain William Hawthorne of the 80th Regiment led troops from his unit as well as a detachment of the Queen's Rangers and one hundred seamen from the HMS *Charon* under Lieutenant Bartholomew James.[9] They landed at Newport News around 7 P.M. and marched to Hampton, a few miles to the east. Guided by a local resident who was pressed into service at one of the houses they passed, the detachment reached Hampton at midnight and commenced a search of the town. Lieutenant James recalled, "We entered the town of Hampton, dividing ourselves in three divisions, and surrounding with a profound silence the chief streets and houses, and taking out of their beds the principal inhabitants."[10]

British commanders attempted to restrain their men from plundering, but had only limited success. Lieutenant James admitted in his journal that "outrages [that were] unavoidable with such a body of men, in the enemy's town in the dead of night," did occur.[11]

By 2 A.M. Captain Hawthorne and Lieutenant James, concerned that the local militia would try to cut their detachment off from their boats if they stayed in Hampton any longer, proceeded back to the ships with a handful of river pilots pressed into service.[12] The officers' concerns were justified; they came under fire on their return and suffered several casualties.[13]

Arnold sent a second detachment ashore on New Year's Eve near the village of Warwick, north of Newport News. A party of militia had been spotted at nightfall along the shore and Arnold wanted to investigate. He sent a detachment of jaegers under Captain Johann Ewald to reconnoiter the area.[14]

Ewald was a bold German commander and veteran of numerous battles in New York, New Jersey, and Pennsylvania, as well as the more recent campaign that captured Charleston, South Carolina. He and his jaegers were well suited to fight the Virginia militia with their open-order style of combat. Maneuverability on the battlefield was essential when fighting an elusive enemy like the American militia, and Ewald's jaegers were possibly the most maneuverable infantry Britain had in America.

Captain Ewald and his jaegers, joined by Captain Althouse's loyalist riflemen from New York, rowed ashore in four boats. They were supported by a detachment of the Queen's Rangers, who followed in their own boats. Ewald described their landing. "I approached within rifle shot, the shore was high. I ordered several shots fired at them, which they answered with small-arms fire, where upon I concluded that they did not have any cannon with them. They were posted behind fences and appeared to number several hundred men."[15] When he realized that the water beneath the boats was only waist-deep, Ewald "called to my men to fire a volley, draw their hunting swords, plunge into the water, and swiftly attack the foe."[16] The bold German captain proudly recalled that "everyone obeyed. The enemy fired a volley when we jumped into the water and three men were wounded. But the enemy was startled by the unexpected attack and withdrew."[17]

Ewald and his men scrambled up the steep bank of the river in pursuit. "I formed my men as well as I could," he recalled, "and took fifty men with me to pursue the enemy."[18] The Virginians, estimated by Ewald to be over two hundred strong, made a stand at a nearby plantation.[19] Undeterred by their numbers, Ewald ordered his men forward, but the militia held their ground. The Queen's Rangers soon came ashore to tip the balance, and the militia withdrew under cover of darkness. Ewald cautiously pushed on into Warwick, where he collected fresh provisions and spent a tense night.[20]

At some point in the operation Arnold came ashore to congratulate Ewald on his success. Arnold "admired the bravery of the men and expressed his heartfelt thanks for my good will," recalled Ewald.[21] Ewald was uninterested in Arnold's praise; he viewed Arnold's order to attack the militia with his jaegers as reckless.

> I do not deny that this little trick left me with no great opinion of General Arnold's judgment, ordering men without bayonets to land and attack an enemy equipped with bayonets since the light infantry [of the 80th Regiment] was just as close to them as I was. That the enemy lost his nerve and left—that was luck! But had they taken a stand, and thrown themselves upon the jagers and [riflemen] when I climbed up the steep bank with my men, which could not be done in the best order, all would have been lost.[22]

Skirmishes resumed at daybreak as rebel militia returned and probed Ewald's force. Ewald received orders to return to the fleet at 9 A.M., but when he reached the shore he found that low tide had forced the boats to remain far offshore, so the tired captain and his men had to wade through the chilly water that eventually rose to their waists. It took the wet and exhausted troops "a good quarter of an hour" to reach the boats, which then transported them to the fleet, still anchored in the river channel.[23]

Arnold proceeded upriver with his transports and several warships, sailing on the flood tide to Hog Island. Along the way they chased and seized several merchant ships loaded with tobacco. One of these ships became grounded in low water along the north bank of the James. When Arnold sent a party to free the vessel, they were fired upon by militia onshore. Arnold sent a flag with a message to the rebels to cease their actions or face the destruction of their town (Warwick): "I have to [tell] you that however disagreeable It may be to me, unless you immediately desist firing, and suffer the Prize [grounded ship] to be taken away with all Her Materials, I shall be under the Necessity of landing and burning the Village, which I wish to avoid."[24]

The militia relented to Arnold's threat and withdrew, trading the stuck ship for the safety of their town.

Not all of Arnold's ships sailed up the James River on New Year's Day. In fact, most of Arnold's warships, including his largest, the HMS *Charon*, remained anchored off Newport News awaiting the arrival of the missing transport ships and guarding against the sudden appearance of the French navy. While they waited for Arnold to return and his missing transports to arrive, several landing parties went ashore on both sides of the James River to forage. Skirmishes ensued with the local militia, and one in particular, near Newport News, cost the British nearly twenty men.[25]

WHILE MOST OF ARNOLD'S ships of war remained anchored in Hampton Roads, his transport ships, escorted by the twenty-four-gun *Hope*, the fourteen-gun *Swift*, and the twelve-gun privateer *Cornwallis*, slowly made their way up the James River.[26] By January 2, Arnold reached Burwell's Ferry, which lay on the north bank of the river about four miles from Williamsburg.

The former capital was in a state of panic.[27] The few men able to bear arms to defend the town were gathered at King's Mill and Burwell's Ferry under General Thomas Nelson and Colonel James Innes. Nathanael Burwell was with the militia at his ferry landing on the James River, and described a bleak situation to Governor Jefferson in Richmond:

> The Enemy's Fleet have just now [arrived] off this Place; they consist of 23 Sail, including two Men of war; a number of Flat bottom'd Boats are a-Stern of the Ships full of men. We have near 200 men under the Command of Colo. Innis and myself a number very insufficient for the present Purpose: however nothing shall be wanting as far as we're able to oppose the Enemy if they attempt to land. A Small Party of Foot and Horse are now engag'd with a Boat detachd from the Fleet.[28]

From Arnold's vantage point on the river, it was difficult to judge the size of the militia force gathered onshore. Ewald described it as "several battalions" strong. Arnold hoped he could once again intimidate the militia and inhabitants into submission with a stern warning, and sent a flag of truce ashore. "Having the honor to command a Body of His Majesty's Troops, sent for the protection of his Loyal Subjects in this country, I am surprised to observe the hostile appearance of the Inhabitants under Arms on the Shore. I have therefore sent Lieut. White, with a Flagg of Truce, to be informed of their intentions. If they are to offer a vain opposition to the Troops under my command, in their landing, they must be answerable for the consequences."[29]

Asserting that he had "not the least intention to injure the peaceable Inhabitants in their persons or property," Arnold pledged that whatever provisions the inhabitants willingly supplied his force "shall be punctually paid for."[30]

General Nelson was not interested in any deal with Arnold. Nelson replied that he "would not and could not give up to a traitor." Furthermore, continued the militia general, "if he were to get hold of Arnold, he would hang him up by the heels, according to the orders of the Congress."[31]

Arnold chose to ignore Nelson's bravado and continued upriver, anchoring off Jamestown Island at nightfall. He apparently intended to send troops ashore the next day, but he reversed himself before they landed when he learned that militia reinforcements had arrived in Williamsburg.[32] Instead, Arnold sailed further up the James River.

On the same day that Nelson rebuffed Benedict Arnold at Burwell's Ferry, Governor Jefferson in Richmond finally learned the extent of the invasion and the danger the mystery fleet (now confirmed to be a British expedition) posed for Virginia. Jefferson sent letters to the county lieutenants of over twenty counties in central Virginia instructing them to muster one quarter of their militia and rendezvous as quickly as possible at Petersburg. The governor also sent letters to the frontier counties of Shenandoah, Rockingham, Augusta, and Rockbridge, instructing a portion of their militia to march with their weapons (preferably rifles) to Richmond.

Jefferson offered a weak explanation for his delay in summoning the militia to Nelson in Williamsburg: "It happened unfortunately that from the Tenor of Mr. Wrays Letter [from December 31, which gave Jefferson the first news of a fleet's arrival], we had reason to expect more precise information within a few hours."[33]

Instead of a few hours, however, it took two days for Jefferson to learn that the unidentified ships were British. Why he was not more proactive in discovering this was never explained by the governor, but upon his discovery that the fleet belonged to the enemy, Jefferson acted, assuring Nelson that "we mean to have four thousand six hundred Militia in the Field," as soon as possible.[34]

Governor Jefferson also turned to General Steuben at Wilton, updating the Continental officer about the enemy fleet and requesting his presence before the executive council in Richmond.[35] Steuben, concerned that the large cache of Continental military stores at Petersburg was the enemy's real target, rushed 150 Continental levies (new recruits) from Chesterfield Courthouse to Petersburg to protect the supplies and help move them to a more secure location.

Before January 2 ended, Jefferson also took measures to transfer the Hessian prisoners who had remained in Charlottesville during the previous British raid northward, and to move the military stores and government records in Richmond to a safe location across the James River.[36] Despite all the activity in and around the capital, a sense of urgency had yet to develop. Jefferson was not even certain that Richmond was a target of the enemy, and even if it was, the British still had to overcome a defensive battery that overlooked the river at one of its narrowest spots: Hood's Point.

About thirty miles downriver from Richmond, high on a one-hundred-foot bluff on the southern bank of the James River where the flow of the river curved sharply from south to northeast, was Hood's Point. It was the strongest defensible position along the entire river—the ideal place to challenge enemy ships struggling upriver against the current. Cannon positioned on the bluff could pound vessels mercilessly as they approached the sharp bend in the river and maintain a deadly and accurate barrage as ships slowed to make the turn and continue upriver (assuming the ships were still afloat). A hastily constructed fort with a battery of three eighteen-pound and one twenty-four-pound iron cannon, plus an eight-inch brass howitzer, had been erected on the bluff in the fall of 1780, but the fort was significantly undermanned (only fifty troops held the works) when Arnold approached with his expedition, and the fortifications were incomplete and open in the rear.[37]

Early in the evening of January 3, Arnold, whose fleet had made excellent progress that day sailing up the river from Jamestown, ordered his transports and warships to anchor in a thick haze about half a mile downriver from Hood's Point. One transport mistakenly continued on and sailed within range of the rebel battery, which promptly opened fire on the vessel. Lieutenant Colonel Simcoe described what happened next. "Upon the first shot the skipper and his people left the deck; when Capt. Murray [of the Queen's Rangers] seized the helm, and the soldiers assisting him, he passed by the fort without any damage from its fire, and anchored above it."[38]

The haze that hung over the river obscured the rest of Arnold's fleet and prompted the militia commander of Hood's Point, Colonel James Cocke, to hold his fire on them. Around 10 P.M., however, the wind picked up and the haze cleared away. Cocke reported that

> we could see their Hulls very plain, at which time we began a Fire of Twice every half hour from One of the Three Guns that we could make Bare on them, which Fire, I intended to keep up, during the night, as I had not the least thought of their attempting to land till near the morning, as the Wind Blew very fresh and made [large waves], which must make it very troublesome for them to Land.[39]

Colonel Cocke sent twenty-five men—half of his garrison—down to the mouth of Ward's Creek, which flowed into the James River about a quarter of a mile downriver from the fortification, to keep watch for an enemy landing.[40]

A shore landing was exactly what Arnold intended. In spite of the ease with which his stray ship had passed Hood's Point (revealing the battery as an ineffective obstacle to the navigation of the river), Arnold decided to neutralize the rebel fort with a ground assault on its rear. He ordered the *Hope* and *Cornwallis* to bombard the fort while troops landed up Ward's Creek and circled around to attack Hood's Point in its open rear. Ewald recalled that a detachment of jaegers, along with Captain Althouse's New York loyalists and two companies of Queen's Rangers, all under Lieutenant Colonel Simcoe, boarded boats and rowed to Ward's Creek.[41] Simcoe remembered the attack differently, crediting 130 of his rangers along with the light infantry and grenadier company of the 80th Regiment with capturing the fort.[42] Simcoe noted, "The landing was effected silently and apparently with secrecy about a mile from the battery, and a circuit was made to surprise its garrison: in the meantime the fleet was fired upon, but ineffectually on account of its distance."[43]

Colonel Cocke's detachment at Ward's Creek spotted the enemy boats making their way up the creek and immediately warned the garrison inside the fort.[44] Cocke later explained that "by their place of landing I was confident that their Intention was to come Round on our Backs and cut off our Retreat. As we then had but about 40 men in the Fort, we thought it was in Vain for us to continue, as we had not the least hopes of defending ourselves, therefore I gave orders for every man to take his arms, and march out of the Fort."[45]

When Simcoe's detachment reached the fort, they found it deserted. After disabling the iron cannon by driving spikes into the touch holes used to prime them, Simcoe returned to the shore with the howitzer.[46]

At the loss of one man aboard ship, who was killed by the fort's "brisk" cannon fire during Simcoe's landing (reportedly twenty shots total), Arnold had neutralized the strongest rebel defensive position on the James River.[47]

Benedict Arnold's fleet remained anchored below Hood's Point until dawn, at which time it resumed its movement upriver, reaching Westover Planation, six miles above Hood's Point around 10 A.M. Westover was the seat of the late William Byrd, the patriarch of one of Virginia's most prominent families. Heavy debt (much of it gambling related) and Tory sympathies caused much angst for Colonel Byrd on the eve of the Revolution, and he escaped from his many pressures in 1776 by committing suicide. His wife, Mary Willing Byrd, a cousin of Benedict Arnold's wife, Peggy Shippen, assumed responsibility for the estate and managed to stave off bankruptcy.

Mrs. Byrd's political sentiments were a mystery to most people. It was probable that, like her husband, she held loyalist sympathies, but if so she was wise enough to keep such sentiments from her neighbors.

When Arnold's fleet anchored directly offshore from her mansion house, Mrs. Byrd found herself with little choice but to play hostess to the British. Her plantation, with its numerous outbuildings, as well as the mansion, became Arnold's base of operation for the next week.

While Mrs. Byrd provided Arnold and his officers with a late breakfast, the British transports emptied their holds of troops, horses, artillery, and supplies. Despite heavy rain, Arnold commenced a march to Richmond, a town of some six hundred inhabitants and the new capital of Virginia, twenty-five miles northwest of Westover, in the late afternoon.[48]

Lieutenant Colonel Simcoe estimated that the column was eight hundred strong, which meant that three to four hundred men were left behind at Westover.[49] Ewald was placed in charge of the advance guard, made up of his jaegers and Captain Althouse's New York loyalist riflemen as well as the light infantry of the Queen's Rangers and thirty mounted Rangers.

Simcoe, with the rest of his cavalry, followed by Lieutenant Colonel Dundas with the 80th Regiment, Colonel Robinson and his Loyal American corps, and four six-pound cannon, comprised the main body. The rear guard trailed behind with an officer and ten mounted Queen's Rangers.[50] The night was very dark due to the heavy rain, and Ewald's advance guard moved cautiously, fearing an ambush. He observed in his diary that there were many excellent spots from which the rebels could have ambushed Arnold's column, but the Virginians failed to take advantage of any of them.

One reason for this was that Arnold's sudden appearance at Westover and subsequent march toward Richmond once again caught Virginia's authorities by surprise. Although the militia had been ordered to muster two days earlier and indeed did so throughout the state, Virginia's leaders were still uncertain of Arnold's destination. In fact, many, including General Steuben, assumed that Arnold intended to march on Petersburg. Thus, Arnold's rapid evening march from Westover toward Richmond gave the Virginians little time to react.

Another reason few militia opposed Arnold's march was that the local forces in the area, namely the Henrico, Charles City, and New Kent County militia, were poorly armed and undersupplied. Benjamin Harrison, a neighbor of Mrs. Byrd at Berkeley Plantation and the county lieutenant of Henrico (not to mention signer of the Declaration of Independence), reported to Governor Jefferson on the afternoon of January 4 that the militia "are assembling fast . . . but many of them are quite without arms of any kind, what they have are mostly unfit for service, to add to this dismal account I must inform you that we have no ammunition of any kind, or so small a quantity that it is scarcely worth naming."[51]

Although they lacked arms and ammunition, Virginia's defenders were not completely inactive. A small party of rebel militia officers reconnoitering the road to Richmond stumbled upon Ewald's advance guard around midnight. Ewald described what happened: "The [rebel] major had gone out to observe exactly where we were in our march. I had marched so quietly that he was quite astonished when several men grabbed his horse by the bridle and knocked him off."[52]

Simcoe had similar good fortune the next morning. After a brief rest at Four Mile Creek (fourteen miles from Westover and eleven miles from Richmond), Arnold's column resumed its march at dawn. They soon arrived at a dismantled bridge. Simcoe, with his mounted rangers of the advance guard, managed to cross the stream, but the bridge had to be repaired for the cannon to cross, so the column halted. During this halt, a party of Virginia militia appeared on the other side of the creek near Arnold's advanced guard. Simcoe described what happened: "Some of the enemy's militia, who had destroyed [the bridge] the evening before, and were to assemble with others to defend it, were deceived by the dress of the Rangers, and came to Lt. Col. Simcoe, who immediately reprimanded them for not coming sooner, held conversation with them, and then sent them prisoners to General Arnold."[53]

The green coats of the Queen's Rangers had confused the militia; they assumed the rangers were fellow rebels, and were much chagrined to discover otherwise when Simcoe announced that they were now prisoners of His Majesty's forces.

Arnold's troops continued their march to Richmond, arriving early in the afternoon of January 5. Arnold wished to make a strong impression upon both the inhabitants and the militia that had assembled in Richmond, so he formed his column in open order (which extended the column and gave it the appearance of being larger than it was).

The small town of Richmond, which had been established in the 1730s near the rapids of the James River, was ringed by a series of very steep hills. When Arnold's column reached the outskirts, one such steep, hundred-foot-high hill loomed before them. Upon it, staring down at Arnold's column, were two to three hundred Virginia militia.[54]

Known today as Church Hill (because the church in which Patrick Henry declared "Give me liberty, or give me death!" sits upon it), the hill was a strong defensible position that commanded the road to Richmond. Arnold and his column had to pass directly beneath it, well within musket range of the rebel militia. Arnold was particularly concerned about the possibility of rebel riflemen hidden in the brush on the hill. He pointed to the overgrown brush and declared to Captain Ewald, "That's a task made for you!"[55] Ewald recalled, "I deployed at once, formed two ranks well dispersed, and climbed up the hill. The enemy left after firing a volley which wounded one jager, but three others who had gone too far to the right were captured."[56]

Ewald and his jaegers inclined to their right on their ascent up the steep hill in an effort to swing around the militia's left flank. A portion of the rebel militia responded by filing to their left to extend their flank, but they were too few, too inexperienced, and too scared to stop Ewald's advance. The frightened militia also faced Simcoe's mounted rangers, who struggled up the hill to the left of Ewald.

The militia on top of the hill withdrew rearward before Ewald's riflemen reached the crest. Many of the Virginians fled into nearby woods "in great confusion," their fight finished for the day.[57] Others crossed a deep ravine in their rear (that cut into Church Hill) and scrambled up the steep embankment to join other militia already posted there.[58] This location, known today as Libby Hill, was essentially a knoll of Church Hill that jutted out toward the river. It overlooked both the road that Arnold's column was on and the flat plateau of Church Hill that Ewald's jaegers had just captured.

Ewald was initially hesitant to charge across the flat, open plateau that stood between the ravine and his position on the eastern edge of Church Hill (known today as Chimborazo Park). "On the whole," Ewald declared in his diary years later, "it was a crucial moment for me. I was on barren, level ground and the enemy could count my men."[59] To make matters worse, Ewald continued, "my men appeared to be so tired and worn out that I no longer dared to rely on their legs for a hurried flight." Ewald opted to "try to detain [the enemy militia] by skirmishing until more troops came up for my support."[60]

Luckily for Ewald and his tired jaegers, Simcoe and his mounted rangers soon appeared on the hill and supported Ewald's left flank. It had been a difficult ascent for Simcoe's horses and their riders—so difficult that the cavalrymen had to dismount and lead their horses up the slope by the bit. "Luckily," remembered Simcoe, "the enemy made no resistance, nor did they fire, but on the cavalry's arrival on the summit [they] retreated to the woods in great confusion."[61]

Simcoe's horsemen benefited from Ewald's aggressive charge up the hill on the right flank minutes earlier; it had driven most of the militia from the plateau. Confronted by both Ewald's jaegers and Simcoe's mounted rangers (who at any moment might swing behind Ewald and charge upon the Virginians' vulnerable left flank—a flank that was not protected by the ravine), the Virginians hastily withdrew from Libby Hill and fled westward.

Ewald led his men down Church Hill and rejoined Arnold's main column on the road while Simcoe and his cavalry trailed the fleeing militia westward. When he reached the western edge of Church Hill, Simcoe's attention was drawn to a party of militia horsemen in the valley below (known today as Shockoe Bottom). The rebel horsemen were focused on Arnold's advancing column down along the river, which was marching straight at them on the road into town. Simcoe attempted to swing his cavalry behind the mounted rebels, but a creek blocked his way, and the rebel horsemen spotted Simcoe's movement and withdrew westward up Shockoe Hill (yet another steep hill that lay across the valley from Church Hill).[62]

Undeterred, Simcoe tried a little deception, presenting himself and his men as fellow militia. Simcoe recalled that, "having crossed [the creek] lower down, [I] ascended the hill, using such conversation and words towards [the militia] as might prevent their inclination to retreat; however, when the Rangers were arrived within twenty yards of the summit, the enemy greatly superior in numbers, but made up of militia, spectators, some with and some without arms, galloped off."[63]

The militia horsemen were not fooled by Simcoe's ruse, and withdrew westward. Simcoe's cavalry pursued, but most rode upon horses still weak from the voyage from New York, so only a handful of rebels were captured.

Upon his return from the pursuit, Simcoe was ordered by Arnold to lead a detachment a few miles west of Richmond to destroy a foundry near the village of Westham on the James River. Westham was the site where Governor Jefferson had sent much of Richmond's military stores and government papers. More importantly, the foundry at Westham was one of the few places in Virginia capable of casting cannon and producing gunpowder. Hundreds of barrels of powder were stored there, as were nearly thirty cannon. The destruction of the foundry and supplies would be a big blow to the rebels.

Arnold sent Simcoe with his corps of rangers, as well as the light infantry and grenadier companies of the 80th Regiment and a detachment of Ewald's jaegers and Althouse's loyalists, to the foundry while he remained in Richmond with the remainder of his force (essentially the 80th Regiment, Robinson's Loyal American Corps, and those soldiers unable to make the march to Westham due to fatigue). Simcoe and his force met no opposition on their march west. When they reached the foundry, about six miles from Richmond, Simcoe tasked Ewald with destroying what he could while he led a hundred men another mile west to the village of Westham. The ever-efficient Ewald recalled that "I . . . tried to attack the [foundry], which lay in a valley close to the left bank of the James River, from all sides. All the people of the foundry fell into my hands. . . . I had left half of the men under arms in the hills, and with the other half I damaged and made unserviceable as much of the machinery and tools found at the smelter as was possible."[64]

Simcoe, who apparently was not present for most of the damage but was informed by subordinates what had been accomplished, noted in his memoirs that "upon consultation with the artillery officer [that accompanied Simcoe's detachment] it was thought better to destroy the magazine than to blow it up, this fatiguing business was effected by carrying the powder down the cliffs, and pouring it into the water; the warehouses and mills were then set on fire, and many explosions happened in different parts of the buildings . . . and the foundry, which was a very complete one, was totally destroyed."[65]

Arnold was very pleased with the raid, reporting to General Clinton that 310 barrels of gunpowder and a large supply of oats had been destroyed (mostly by dumping it in the James River), as well as the cannon foundry and 26 cannon.[66]

Although the Virginia militia had thus far offered little opposition to Arnold's troops, Simcoe and Ewald were both eager to return to Richmond as soon as possible. Both officers worried that every hour that passed increased the possibility of enemy reinforcements cutting their detachment off from Richmond, so they commenced their march back to the rebel capital at 10 P.M.

Ewald's troops were apparently not as concerned about the enemy as their commander was, for Ewald complained that many of his men marched back to Richmond drunk, having found a large supply of wine and beer near the foundry. "I assembled my men at once, of whom two thirds were drunk because large stores of wine and beer had been found in the houses. They were now so noisy that one could hear us two hours away."[67]

The entire detachment reached Richmond incident free well after midnight, at which point many of the men literally collapsed from fatigue and slept in the numerous abandoned buildings of the city.

ARNOLD'S MEN WERE NOT the only ones fatigued by the day's activities. Governor Jefferson spent much of January 5 on horseback, riding from Tuckahoe—his boyhood home located about ten miles west of Richmond, where he had sent his wife and three daughters—to Westham to superintend the removal of arms and supplies across the river, and then to Manchester, a town directly across from Richmond, where Jefferson observed Arnold's troops entering the city. The governor did not stay long in Manchester; he wished to confer with Steuben, so he rode along the south side of the James River in search of the general, but could not locate him. Late in the day a messenger from Richmond reached Jefferson with a proposal from General Arnold to spare much of the capital from destruction. Arnold described his offer to his superior, General Clinton.

> On my arrival at Richmond I was informed there was in stores a large quantity of tobacco, West India goods, wines, sailcloth, etc. There were between 30 and 40 sail of vessels loaded with tobacco between Westover and Richmond. As the navigation of the river above Westover was intricate, the season critical, and many difficulties attending the removal of the goods, a proposal was made to the merchants who remained at Richmond to prevent the destruction of private property . . . that upon their delivering the whole of the enumerated goods on board His Majesty's fleet in the James River, that one-half the value should be paid to them.[68]

It was an audacious proposal, especially coming from the infamous American traitor. If Richmond's merchants delivered their goods, as well as the ships loaded with tobacco in the James River, to Arnold by the following morning, he would pay them half of the value of the goods and spare the town.

Many of the merchants were tempted by this offer, no doubt concluding that something was better than nothing for their property; they forwarded Arnold's proposal to Governor Jefferson for his approval. Jefferson refused to ransom the safety of Richmond and flatly rejected Arnold's offer.[69] The thought of cooperating with the infamous traitor was unacceptable.

Although resistance to Arnold in Virginia had thus far been weak and ineffective, Jefferson was informed on January 5 in a letter from Steuben that nearly one thousand militia had assembled in Petersburg. Only four hundred carried arms, but more weapons were being sent to them on the assumption that Petersburg would be Arnold's next target. Steuben also reported that he had ordered approximately

150 newly raised Virginia Continentals meant for General Greene's army in the Carolinas to join the militia in Petersburg.[70]

The shortage of weapons among the militia at Petersburg also existed on the north side of the James River. Large bodies of militia gathered near Westham and southeast of Richmond in New Kent County under General Nelson, but in both cases gun and powder shortages significantly limited their effectiveness. Jefferson, Steuben, Nelson, and others did all they could to find weapons for the men, but the confusion caused by Arnold's rapid march to Richmond and the destruction of the supplies at the Westham foundry and in Richmond significantly hampered these efforts.

Benedict Arnold reacted to Jefferson's rejection of his offer to spare Richmond by unleashing his troops on the capital. Arnold recalled that

> I found myself under the disagreeable necessity of ordering a large quantity of rum to be stove, several warehouses of salt to be destroyed; several public storehouses and smith's shops with their contents were consumed by the flames; a very fine rope-walk full of materials, private property, was burnt without my orders by an officer who was informed it was public property; a large magazine with quartermaster's stores, sailcloath was burnt; a printing press and types were also purified by the flames.[71]

An inventory of the public property damaged or destroyed by Arnold's troops in Richmond and Westham included 2,200 small arms, 4,000 French musket locks in two casks, and nearly 40 cannon, ranging from thirty-two- to four-pounders. Over seven thousand solid-shot cannon rounds and twenty thousand grapeshot rounds were tossed in the river, 503 hogsheads of rum stove in on the capital streets, and two warehouses full of salt were burned to the ground. Five six-pound French brass cannon were spared from destruction and seized by Arnold.[72]

Private property was apparently not immune to seizure, either. Captain Ewald claimed that "forty-two vessels were loaded with all kinds of merchandise for the corps' booty and sailed down the James

River."[73] Some of the merchandise loaded aboard the ships was undoubtedly the plunder Arnold's troops had taken from the many abandoned homes and buildings in Richmond.[74] Much of it was also seized tobacco.

By noon of January 6, Arnold was ready to depart Richmond and return to Westover. Trudging through driving rain that turned the road into a quagmire, Arnold's men had great trouble on the march. Lieutenant Colonel Simcoe recalled that "the roads were rendered by the rain slippery and difficult, and in most places were narrow and overhung by bushes, so that the troops were frequently obliged to march by files, which made it impossible for the officers, who were on foot, to see far before them, and to take their customary precautions."[75]

Simcoe claimed that nine of his rangers, either overcome by fatigue or the desire to desert, were taken by the rebels on the march back. Ewald claimed that, "since the march back took place rather hastily, some sixty men—too fatigued to keep up—fell into the hands of the [rebels]."[76]

The expedition halted in the early evening at Four Mile Creek, only eleven miles outside of Richmond. Most of Arnold's men were exhausted, and all were wet and miserable as they camped without any cover from the cold driving rain. They endured the night and resumed their march to Westover at sunrise.

Parties of militia hovered on their rear, but none attacked Arnold's force; the very storm that tormented Arnold's men prevented General Thomas Nelson from striking Arnold. Nelson explained to Jefferson how Arnold escaped a blow from the militia troops under his command: "Even the Elements have conspired to favour [the enemy]. On Saturday Night [January 6] I intended a Blow at their Rear, when the Gates of Heaven were opened, and such a Flood of Rain poured down as rendered my Plan abortive by almost drowning the Troops, who were in Bush Tents, and by injuring their Arms and Ammunition so much that they were quite unfit for Service."[77]

Had Nelson been able to attack, it is unlikely he would have inflicted much damage on Arnold's force. The militia commander had at most four hundred poorly armed troops, just half of Arnold's force.[78] As a result, there was little, besides poor weather, to stop

Arnold and his men from reaching Westover unscathed on January 7.

A day after Arnold's return to Westover, a party of militia was observed on the heights east of Westover, overlooking Herring Creek. Arnold, uncertain of the size and proximity of the rebel militia, ordered Simcoe to patrol towards Long Bridge, north of Westover, to investigate.

Simcoe led forty mounted rangers, supported by two companies of his infantry under Ewald, northward after dark.[79] They had only gone a couple of miles when Simcoe's lead rider, Sergeant Kelly, was challenged by two rebel horsemen on the road. The quick-witted sergeant approached the rebels in as friendly a manner as he could, then rushed at them, grabbing one rebel and frightening the other off his horse and into the bushes.[80] A runaway slave whom the two rebels had intercepted earlier in the evening was freed, and he readily cooperated with Simcoe. From the liberated slave and the captured rebel, Simcoe learned that a large party of militia had gathered at Charles City Courthouse, about nine miles from Westover.

Led by the grateful runaway slave, who directed Simcoe along a little-used path to Charles City, Simcoe's detachment approached the outskirts of the village. One of Simcoe's officers, a Lieutenant Holland, who was similar in size to the captured rebel horseman, led the column and was challenged by a mounted rebel sentry near the village who called out in the dark at their approach: "Who goes there"? Simcoe described what happened next: "Lt. Holland answered, 'A friend,' gave the countersign procured from the prisoner, 'It is I, me, Charles,' the name of the person he personated."[81]

The ruse worked, and the rebel horseman allowed Lieutenant Holland, accompanied by Kelly, to approach. Before the lone militiaman realized his mistake, Sergeant Kelly drew his weapon upon him and announced that he was a prisoner. Simcoe's men continued forward and encountered another rebel vidette (mounted sentry), who managed to escape an attempt to overpower him and ride off, firing his weapon to warn the militia at Charles City Courthouse. Simcoe recalled that "the advance division immediately rushed on, and soon arrived at the Court-house; a confused and scattered firing began on all sides."[82]

The shock of the sudden attack, combined with the darkness of the evening, which only heightened the fear of the militia, prevented the militia from organizing an effective defense, and instead they fled in all directions. Simcoe was satisfied to let them flee, not wishing to reveal his true strength by staying at the courthouse too long. The rangers gathered up their prisoners and headed back to Westover. Simcoe reported one ranger killed and three wounded. British estimates of the militia losses were twenty to thirty killed and wounded, in addition to nearly twenty prisoners taken.[83] American accounts claimed just a handful of losses and downplayed the incident.[84] Whatever the true American casualties were, the fact remained that a small British patrol surprised and routed a larger militia force at Charles City Courthouse.

The good news continued for Arnold the following day with the arrival of his missing transport ships carrying four hundred reinforcements. Separated by a gale in December, the ships had finally caught up with the expedition. Their stay at Westover was brief, however, for Arnold decided on January 10 to embark for Portsmouth.

Arnold's preparations to depart were observed across the river by Steuben, who moved a force of approximately eight hundred militia from Petersburg further south to Prince George Courthouse in anticipation of Arnold's departure. Steuben concluded that refortifying Hood Point was impracticable, but he speculated that since Arnold could not be certain of this, the British commander would send troops ashore to investigate before his fleet passed the point. Steuben decided to lay an ambush for the expected landing party. He explained his actions to General Greene, the commander of the American Southern army in the Carolinas: "Thinking it very probable [that Arnold] would land a party to examine [the] works [at Hood's] before they attempted to pass, I ordered 300 Infantry & about 30 Horse under Col. Clark to lay in Ambush to receive them."[85]

Colonel Clark was likely George Rogers Clark of Vincennes fame, who had recently arrived in Richmond from the Western frontier. Clark was pressed into service, and set up a strong ambush point to strike at Arnold's troops on their march southward.

Accounts of Clark's ambush near Hood's Point vary. Steuben, who was not actually present at the ambush, claimed that Arnold's troops began landing near Hood's Point at dusk. Arnold reported that he sent 350 troops ashore under Simcoe at 7 P.M. (which was well past dusk) with orders to march to a crossroad two miles inland and attack the enemy that was reportedly there.[86] Simcoe claimed his troops landed at night and that General Arnold wanted Simcoe to surprise a detachment of rebels at Bland's Mill, a few miles inland.[87] The person that actually led the advance of Simcoe's detachment, at least initially, Captain Johann Ewald, reported that they landed at 10 P.M. on Hood's Point with no opposition.[88] Ewald recalled in his diary, "I was the first to go ashore. Since the thunderstorm had subsided and a beautiful, clear evening with moonlight followed, by which one could see far around, I took four men, a horn blower, and Captain Murray of the rangers to reconnoiter and patrol a short distance into the country. I ordered two men to proceed in front of me at a distance of fifty paces, and I followed with the people mentioned."[89]

About five hundred paces up the wide, sandy road, Ewald suddenly heard horses approaching. He recalled,

I had no desire to run back, since I thought that it would be several men whom I could seize. To the right on this side of [a] fence, or railing, I found three or four trees, behind which I concealed myself and the other four men. A moment later, a body of twenty or thirty horse appeared. I had in mind to let them pass and fire upon them from the rear. But the officer, who looked my way just as he approached me, ordered a halt and called to me, "Who's there?" I kept still; he called again, "Who's there?" Since the game was now too serious for me, I jumped out from behind the tree and shouted to him, "Friend of the watch!" At that moment I called for fire. The two jagers who were with me, and the horn blower, who was armed with one of my double pistols, gave fire and the entire troop fled. The two jagers whom I had sent ahead [had] dropped to the ground at [the enemy's] approach and contributed their fire.[90]

Frustrated that he had not taken more troops with him (which, he insisted, would have enabled him to capture the enemy horsemen), Ewald returned to the shore to report to Arnold. He found the rest of the landing party, about 200 troops of the 80th Regiment, ashore and the whole detachment, 550 strong, ready to march.

Simcoe pulled Ewald aside and informed him that Colonel Robinson's Loyal American Corps, instead of Ewald and his jaegers, would be the advance guard. Simcoe "begged me not to take offense," Ewald recalled, and the German officer attributed the decision to Arnold's desire to give Robinson "an opportunity to get his name in the *Gazette*."[91] Ewald's 50 jaegers trailed behind Robinson's advance guard, which was 170 strong. Behind the jaegers came Simcoe's rangers (120 strong) and, finally, 200 troops from the 80th Regiment.[92]

Ewald noted that the detachment had marched along the road for about a half hour when approximately twenty musket shots were fired toward the head of the column. No one was injured, and the column soon resumed its march. Ewald provided a detailed description of what happened next:

> After . . . about a half an hour, we heard two extraordinary loud voices challenge the head with a very clear "Who—is—there?" The good [Colonel] ordered, "Forward!" At that instant, a terrible fire fell out of the woods from the front and left among Robinson's honorable Americans. Weeping, wailing, and gnashing of teeth arose, and one captain, two officers, and some forty men were either killed or seriously wounded. I ran to the head and found a deplorable situation: the honorable fellows were so disconcerted by their bad luck that if the enemy party had suddenly attacked them with the bayonet, the entire column certainly would have been thrown back to Hood's Point.[93]

Although the ambush was clearly devastating to Robinson's corps, other accounts described a less chaotic situation. Arnold reported that after the heavy fire of the militia Robinson's men "charged the enemy with such firmness and resolution that [the enemy] instantly fled on all sides."[94] Simcoe gave a similar account, and a report in one loyalist gazette claimed that after the militia fired their volley they "ran away, leaving hats, wigs, Etc. Etc. behind them."[95]

Ewald, frustrated at what he viewed as unnecessary losses due to incompetence, snapped at Arnold when he appeared at the head of the column to survey the damage. "So it goes when a person wants to do something that he doesn't understand!" declared Ewald.[96] Arnold ignored Ewald's biting comment and "courteously" requested the German captain take command of the advance guard. The 80th Regiment remained behind to tend to the wounded while the rest of the column resumed its march, but after another thirty minutes Arnold reversed direction, and the column marched back to the river, throwing the damaged rebel cannon from their previous attack on Hood Point into the river in frustration and reboarding their ships.

The next day was rather uneventful. Arnold's fleet slowly made its way downriver, stopping at Cobham (across from Jamestown) on January 12. Approximately one hundred Surry County militia vainly attempted to repel a landing party under Colonel Dundas of the 80th Regiment that was four times their size, but the militia only managed to wound three men before they were forced to withdraw.[97] Dundas burned a warehouse full of flour and seized sixty hogsheads of tobacco. After another uneventful day on the river, General Arnold anchored off of Isle of Wight County on January 14 and disembarked his entire army about twelve miles northwest of Smithfield. Arnold's ultimate destination was Portsmouth, some thirty miles away.

Virginia's military leaders, led by Steuben, struggled to keep up with Arnold's movements. Their efforts were hampered by the scattered nature of the militia (deployed on both sides of the James River) and by the severe shortage of weapons and equipment for the troops. Steuben was actually pleased with the strong turnout of militia, but discouraged by their lack of arms and gear. "Large Numbers of Men are hourly Crowding to this place destitute of Arms," Steuben wrote to Jefferson on January 12 from the vicinity of Hood's Point.[98] Many of the unarmed men looked to Steuben for weapons and orders, but he declined to take responsibility for them until they were properly armed by the state.

The approximately seven hundred militia troops that were armed and under Steuben's command south of the James River were ordered to march from Hood's Point to Cabin Point, just a few miles farther south, on January 13. By then, however, Arnold and his troops were well out of reach of Steuben; it fell to Colonel Josiah Parker and the militia of the lower counties to confront Benedict Arnold.

Colonel Parker was an experienced commander who had led militia troops in battle at Great Bridge in 1775 and Continental troops from 1776 to 1778 as colonel of the 4th Virginia Regiment. A veteran of the Battles of Trenton, Princeton, Brandywine, and Germantown, Parker was an outstanding leader whom Steuben confidently tapped to command the militia in Isle of Wight, Nansemond, Princess Anne, and Norfolk Counties. Although Colonel Parker was unable to challenge Arnold's advance into Smithfield, he hoped to make Arnold pay when he marched on to Portsmouth. Parker established a defensive position with approximately two hundred militia and two cannon a few miles south of Smithfield on the road to Portsmouth.[99]

Parker's position was a strong one. His men defended a dismantled bridge that crossed Cypress Creek, a narrow but deep obstacle on the road to Portsmouth. The banks of both sides of the creek were steep, and access to the bridge passed through a narrow defile that Parker covered with two cannon. The dismantled bridge also served as a dam, which formed an impassible mill pond on the west side of the bridge. This allowed Parker to concentrate most of his force and cannon upon high ground to the east of the bridge. The mill, which sat just to the right of the bridge, was also used by the militia for cover.

On the morning of January 16, Simcoe and his cavalry rode out of Smithfield, discovered Parker's position at Mackie's Mill, and sent word back to Arnold, who ordered Captain Ewald and his jaegers— along with three companies of Simcoe's rangers—to reinforce Simcoe. As the task of dislodging the rebels was better suited for the infantry than cavalry, it appears that Simcoe gave Ewald the responsibility of driving the rebels out. Ewald recalled in his diary that "the enemy had placed his infantry and two [cannon] in the gardens in such a way that they could enfilade the bridge and a great distance on our side. There was much to reconnoiter, but no time for it; we saw the enemy right before our eyes. He had to be driven out, and we immediately proceeded quickly to the task."[100]

Ewald posted thirty jaegers on the high ground near the road behind trees. Half were ordered to keep a constant fire on the cannon
crews; the other half, on the militia in the gardens. "I distributed the
remaining jaegers [among Simcoe's rangers] along the creek and ordered them to fire continuously at anyone who showed himself," recalled Ewald.[101] The rifle fire of the jaegers quickly took effect on the
rebels, and after only four cannon shots (two of solid ball and two
of grape) the rebel guns were withdrawn.[102] Ewald smugly speculated
that the reason the cannon were pulled back from the fight so quickly
was that the crews serving them had no more desire to load them in
the face of the heavy rifle fire of the jaegers.

In the midst of this firefight, Ewald learned about the existence
of a foot bridge over the creek about a thousand paces to his left. He
hurried to investigate and, upon confirmation, ordered ten or twelve
men to cross over. "This had the effect of causing the enemy to abandon the gardens and hedges, and it looked as though he intended to
withdraw to the wood lying behind him," Ewald claimed. "To my
astonishment, however, all the jaegers and rangers left their posts
[near the dismantled bridge] rushed to the footbridge and crossed it,
without my being able to prevent it."[103]

Ewald managed to restore some order to his troops, but no further
advantage was gained because the militia "was so surprised by the
spirit of the men that [they] ran head over heels to the woods."[104]
Ewald claimed the rebels left eleven dead and eight wounded men
who joined eight other unscathed prisoners. Two jaegers and a
Queen's Ranger were also killed in the fight, and five other Crown-
force soldiers were wounded.[105]

With the crossing point secured and the bridge soon repaired,
Arnold and the rest of his corps crossed Cypress Creek the next day.
The remainder of their march to Portsmouth was incident free, and
early in the morning of January 19 Simcoe's cavalry entered the
largely deserted town.

It had been an extremely arduous yet profitable three weeks for
Arnold and his expedition. At the loss of less than a hundred men,
Arnold's force had wreaked havoc and destruction all along the
James River. Virginia's inability to mount an adequate defense against
such a relatively small enemy force exposed the state to ridicule, and

Virginia's leaders chafed at the thought that the traitor Arnold was the cause of this. As Arnold fortified Portsmouth for what looked like a long occupation, Jefferson, Steuben, Nelson, and the rest of Virginia's patriots hoped for a chance at redemption. They soon learned that another Virginian had earned just such redemption in mid-January on a battlefield in South Carolina.

Three

A Difficult Winter
for Both Sides

JANUARY–FEBRUARY 1781

T HE CLOSING MONTHS OF 1780 WERE DISAPPOINTING FOR
General Charles Cornwallis in South Carolina. Harassed in the
low country by rebel militia led by Thomas Sumter and Francis Marion and stung by Ferguson's defeat at Kings Mountain, Cornwallis
abandoned his efforts to subdue North Carolina and retreated to
Winnsboro, South Carolina, where he waited impatiently for General
Leslie's 2,200 reinforcements to arrive from Virginia.

Cornwallis likely found some comfort in the fact that his primary
adversary in the South, General Nathanael Greene of Rhode Island
(who replaced General Horatio Gates as commander of the American
Southern army in early December), found himself in a much worse
situation. General Greene inherited an American army in Charlotte,
North Carolina, that was no match for Cornwallis. Greene's best
troops were roughly 1,400 Maryland and Delaware Continentals.
They were augmented by hundreds of militia and about one hundred
cavalry. Although the American victory at Kings Mountain two

months earlier had bolstered American morale, Greene's troops were in very poor condition. The American commander complained to Governor Jefferson in early December that "the appearance of the troops was wretched beyond description, and their distress, on account of [lack of] provisions, was little less than their suffering for want of clothing and other necessities."[1]

General Greene addressed his supply crisis boldly. He divided his army in the face of a superior enemy. Greene led the bulk of his army to Cheraw Hill, South Carolina, which placed them in position to threaten the important British outpost at Camden (and moved them further away from the threat of Cornwallis in Winnsboro). To counter the appearance that he was retreating, Greene sent Brigadier General Daniel Morgan of Virginia with six hundred men in the opposite direction to threaten the crucial British outpost of Ninety-Six.

Daniel Morgan's heroics at Quebec in 1775 and Saratoga in 1777 (both under Benedict Arnold) had earned him universal acclaim as a bold and courageous commander, but fatigue and discouragement at the lack of promotion caused Morgan to resign from the American army in 1779. The string of American defeats in South Carolina in 1780 prompted Congress to recall Morgan at his desired rank, and when he joined the dispirited Southern army in the fall he received command of the army's corps of light infantry.

On December 21, Brigadier General Morgan led his light corps of nearly four hundred Continentals, one hundred militia, and one hundred cavalry west to link up with additional militia and threaten the British outpost at Ninety-Six near the South Carolina–Georgia border.[2]

Cornwallis responded to Morgan's movement by ordering Lieutenant Colonel Banastre Tarleton and his legion of dragoons and infantry (bolstered by additional infantry detachments from several British regiments) to reinforce Ninety-Six. Tarleton and his men had developed a fierce reputation for their bold—some would say brutal—tactics, and Tarleton's force of 1,100 men was a powerful counter-measure to Morgan.[3] Tarleton positioned his detachment to screen Ninety-Six, but soon realized that General Morgan did not intend to strike the outpost. Never one to avoid a fight, Tarleton marched north to confront Morgan.

Aware that Cornwallis, who had been reinforced with 1,500 troops from Leslie's recently arrived force, posed a serious threat on his flank, Morgan withdrew northwest, away from Tarleton and Cornwallis. On January 16, Morgan halted at a large field south of the Broad River known as the Cowpens, resolved to stand and fight Tarleton if necessary. Morgan spent much of the evening with his men, going from campfire to campfire to inspire them for the impending fight. One soldier who witnessed Morgan's efforts recalled:

> It was upon this occasion I was more perfectly convinced of Gen. Morgan's qualifications to command militia, than I had ever before been. He went among the volunteers, helped them fix their swords, joked with them about their sweet-hearts, told them to keep in good spirits, and the day would be ours. And long after I laid down, he was going about among the soldiers encouraging them, and telling them that the old wagoner would crack his whip over Ben. [Tarleton] in the morning, as sure as they lived. 'Just hold up your heads, boys, three fires,' he would say, 'and you are free, and then when you return to your homes, how the old folks will bless you, and the girls kiss you, for your gallant conduct!' I don't believe he slept a wink that night![4]

MORGAN'S BATTLE PLAN at Cowpens involved a defense in depth comprising three battle lines. He placed approximately 150 militia riflemen in a skirmish line that extended across the road from which Tarleton was expected to approach.[5] The skirmishers deployed in loose order behind trees and were ordered to "feel the enemy as he approached."[6] When pressed, the riflemen were to withdraw to the flanks of the next American line 150 yards in their rear.[7]

Morgan's second line also stretched across the road but in a much tighter formation, the men standing nearly shoulder to shoulder in two ranks. This militia line consisted of three hundred troops divided into four battalions.[8] Morgan expected each battalion to fire at least two volleys before they retreated to the third and final American line.

Morgan's third line consisted of his best troops—Maryland, Delaware, and Virginia Continentals under Lieutenant Colonel John

Howard of Maryland. They were augmented by a few companies of seasoned militia from Virginia and North Carolina. This third line was formed about 150 yards behind the militia line and numbered about 550. In reserve, behind the third line, waited 120 Continental and militia cavalry under Lieutenant Colonel William Washington of Virginia.[9] A few of Washington's horsemen were detached and posted three miles in advance of Cowpens to warn of Tarleton's approach.

Lieutenant Colonel Tarleton approached Cowpens early in the morning of January 17. He commanded approximately 1,100 men, including over 300 cavalry and 750 infantry troops. Tarleton also had two three-pound artillery pieces.[10] Tarleton's force confronted Morgan's cavalry pickets before sunrise and pressed forward, reaching Cowpens at dawn. The Americans were deployed and waiting for him. Thomas Young, a militiaman attached to Washington's cavalry, recalled: "The morning . . . was bitterly cold . . . About sunrise, the British line advanced at a sort of trot with a loud halloo. It was the most beautiful line I ever saw. When they shouted, I heard Morgan say, 'They give us the British halloo, boys. Give them the Indian halloo, by G—!' and he galloped along the lines, cheering the men and telling them not to fire until we could see the whites of their eyes."[11]

Tarleton's dragoons screened his main body and engaged Morgan's riflemen in the skirmish line, but failed to dislodge them. Undeterred, Tarleton ordered his entire force forward. His troops dropped their extra gear and formed a battle line across the road. As they advanced in open order toward the American riflemen they were peppered with "a heavy & galling fire."[12] A few British soldiers responded with unauthorized shots, but most held their fire and continued forward, driving the riflemen back to the militia line.

As Tarleton's force approached within fifty yards of the next American line, each militia battalion unleashed a well-aimed volley into their ranks. A British officer noted that "the effect of the fire was considerable, it produced something like a recoil."[13] Despite the heavy fire, Tarleton's men pressed on and forced the militia to retreat before most had a chance to fire a second time. As the militia withdrew to the third line, some were suddenly attacked by Tarleton's cavalry. Only the timely arrival of Lieutenant Colonel Washington's horsemen saved the panic-stricken militia from disaster.

While Washington engaged Tarleton's cavalry on the American left flank, Morgan's men on the third line braced to engage Tarleton's infantry. The British troops briefly halted to dress their line and close ranks, and then resumed their attack. Morgan proudly noted that the approaching enemy was "received [by] a well-directed and incessant Fire," from the Continentals.[14] The British responded in kind. Tarleton observed, "The fire on both sides was well supported, and produced much slaughter."[15] Another participant noted that both sides "maintained their ground with great bravery; and the conflict . . . was obstinate and bloody."[16]

Tarleton tried to break the deadlock by striking at Morgan's right flank. This key position in the American line was held by a company of Virginia Continentals under Captain Andrew Wallace. They were supported by a party of North Carolina riflemen along the woods to their right. Tarleton sent in his cavalry and reserve battalion of infantry and hit the American right flank hard.

Tarleton's dragoons scattered the American riflemen and were about to gain Captain Wallace's rear when Lieutenant Colonel Washington's cavalry suddenly appeared from the other end of the line and stopped them cold. Although Tarleton's horsemen were forced to retire, his infantry still threatened to turn Morgan's right flank, so Lieutenant Colonel John Howard, commander of the Continental troops, ordered an adjustment in the American line. Unfortunately, Howard's orders were misunderstood, and some confusion occurred in their execution. He explained after the battle: "Seeing my right flank was exposed to the enemy, I attempted to change the front of Wallace's company. In doing this, some confusion ensued, and first a part and then the whole of the company commenced a retreat. The officers along the line seeing this and supposing that orders had been given for a retreat, faced their men about and moved off."[17]

Morgan was initially upset by the unauthorized withdrawal, but Lieutenant Colonel Howard assured him that the battle was not lost.[18] Morgan recalled that "we retired in good Order about 50 Paces, formed, advanced on the Enemy & gave them a fortunate Volley which threw them into Disorder."[19]

In truth, Tarleton's men were disordered prior to the American volley. The initial withdrawal of the American third line prompted the British to rush forward. "They are coming on like a mob," Washington told Howard. "Give them a fire and I will charge them."[20] Howard did precisely that, ordering his men to face about. "In a minute we had a perfect line," recalled Howard.[21] He continued, "The enemy were now very near us. Our men commenced a very destructive fire, which they little expected, and a few rounds occasioned great disorder in their ranks. While in this confusion, I ordered a charge with the bayonet, which order was obeyed with great alacrity."[22]

Morgan proudly described the impact of the American bayonet charge to General Greene: "Lt. Colonel Howard observing [the enemy's disorder] gave orders for the Line to charge Bayonets, which was done with such Address that they fled with the utmost Precipitation, leaving the Field Pieces in our Possession. We pushed our Advantage so effectually, that they never had an Opportunity of rallying."[23]

Tarleton's defeat at Cowpens was nearly total. His detachment was shattered, and he lost over eight hundred men.[24] Only Tarleton and his horsemen escaped.

GENERAL MORGAN REALIZED that despite his decisive victory over Tarleton at Cowpens, his light corps was still in danger from Cornwallis and the main British army of nearly 2,500 men to the east. Morgan therefore immediately commenced a march northward. His objective was twofold: to move the hundreds of British prisoners out of reach of Cornwallis, and to reunite with Greene as fast as possible. Cornwallis, whose army lay between Morgan and Greene, strove to stop Morgan on both counts, and commenced a pursuit of the American light corps.

As Morgan marched into North Carolina, most of the Georgia and South Carolina militia that were with him departed. On January 23, Morgan's force crossed the Catawba River. The British prisoners continued on toward Virginia under the guard of the Virginia militia, who were themselves returning home. That left Morgan with less than four hundred Continentals, Washington's cavalry, and a handful of North Carolina militia, yet Morgan made the bold decision to stand his ground at the Catawba River in North Carolina, await instructions from Greene, and hope for militia reinforcements.[25] Morgan guarded the fords of the Catawba for over a week waiting for Cornwallis to advance and patriot militia to arrive. Both were slow to do so.

Hampered by a large baggage train and heavy rain that flooded the creeks and rivers and turned the roads into a quagmire, Lord Cornwallis's pursuit of Morgan initially progressed at a crawl. In frustration, Cornwallis took the extreme measure of destroying most of his baggage and wagons. This allowed him to quicken his pace, but when he finally reached the Catawba River he found it unfordable due to recent rains. Cornwallis impatiently waited for the flooded river to recede, which it finally did on January 31.

Defending the crossing points against Cornwallis's army were Morgan's Continental and cavalry troops and eight hundred North Carolina militia who had arrived during the week under General William Davidson.[26] A large detachment of these men, led by General Davidson himself, fiercely resisted a late-night British crossing at Cowans Ford. Cornwallis described the crossing in a letter to Lord George Germain.

> Full of confidence in the zeal and gallantry of Brigadier-general O'Hara [and his men] I ordered them to . . . [cross the river and] not to fire until they gained the opposite bank. Their behavior justified my high opinion of them; for a constant fire from the enemy, in a ford upwards of five hundred yards wide, in many places up to their middle, with a rocky bottom and strong current, made no impression on their cool and determined valour, nor checked their passage.[27]

Davidson's men inflicted scores of casualties on the British, but failed to halt their crossing. As the British reached the other side of the river, Davidson's militia fled eastward. They did so without their commander, who was killed in the engagement.

The British crossing at Cowans Ford left Morgan, who had been joined a day earlier by Greene and a small escort of dragoons, with no option but to withdraw northeast through Salisbury and across the Yadkin River.

Three days earlier, Greene had abruptly left his main army on the Pee Dee River (one hundred miles to the east) and rushed westward to confer with Morgan. Upon his arrival, Greene sent word back to General Isaac Huger to send the army's heavy baggage northward to Guilford Courthouse and march the rest of the army towards Salisbury to unite with Morgan.

As General Huger marched northwestward, a bit of good fortune shined on Morgan and his outnumbered men. With Cornwallis across the Catawba River and in pursuit, Morgan's troops crossed the Yadkin River just before heavy rains flooded it and stranded Cornwallis on the other side. Morgan halted his retreat and impatiently waited on the east bank of the river for reinforcements. While he did so, Morgan grudgingly succumbed to a health problem that had plagued him for weeks. Exhausted and in extreme pain due to sciatica, Morgan used the delay in Cornwallis's pursuit to relinquish command of the light corps and return to Virginia to recuperate. Greene took charge of Morgan's men and decided they were too few to defend the receding Yadkin River. He led the light corps and militia further north towards Guilford Courthouse, and united with General Huger and the rest of the American Southern army on February 9.

General Greene immediately held a war council, where it was revealed that his army comprised only 1,426 ill-clad and poorly armed Continentals and 600 poorly armed militia.[28] Approximately thirty miles west of Guilford Courthouse were Cornwallis and 2,500 troops eager to catch the Americans and avenge Cowpens. Greene and his officers agreed that it would be best to avoid an engagement with Cornwallis until they were reinforced by more militia, so Greene ordered a retreat to the Dan River in Virginia. Greene instructed the light infantry corps, now under the command of Colonel Otho Williams of Maryland and increased to seven hundred troops, to screen the army during its retreat northward. Colonel Williams was a veteran officer and an excellent choice to command the light corps in the absence of General Morgan.

Before he departed for the Dan River with the bulk of the army, Greene wrote to General Washington and updated him on the situation.

Lord Cornwallis has been constantly in pursuit of the Light Infantry and the prisoners . . . and [is] still pushing into the country with great rapidity. The moment I was informed of the movements of Lord Cornwallis I put the army in motion on Pedee and . . . set out to join the Light Infantry in order to collect the Militia and embarrass the enemy 'till we could effect a junction of our forces. . . . Heavy rains, deep creeks, bad roads, poor horses and broken harnesses as well as delays for want of provisions prevented our forming a junction as early as I expected, and fearing that the river might fall so as to be fordable, I ordered the army to file off to this place [Guilford Courthouse].[29]

Greene expressed disappointment in the militia turnout, and presented a bleak picture of the army.

We have no provisions but what we receive from our daily collections. Under these circumstances I called a council who unanimously advised to avoid an action and to retire beyond the [Dan River] immediately. . . . I have formed a light army composed of the cavalry . . . and the Legion amounting to 240, a detachment of 280 Infantry under Lt. Col. Howard, the Infantry of Lt. Col. Lee's legion and 60 Virginia Rifle Men making in their whole 700 Men which will be ordered with the Militia to harass the enemy in their advance, check their progress and if possible give us an opportunity to retire without a general action.[30]

WHILE GREENE and the main body of the American army retreated northeast toward the Dan River, Colonel Otho Williams's seven-hundred-man light corps marched northwest in an effort to draw the British away from Greene's main body. Greene had made arrangements to gather boats in the vicinity of Irwin's and Boyd's ferries on the Dan River in Virginia, but he needed time to reach the river and transport his army and its baggage across. Colonel Williams hoped to provide Greene with that time by drawing Cornwallis off in the wrong direction. First, he had to find Cornwallis and get him to pursue. This was achieved on February 11. Williams informed Greene of the encounter: "Accident informed me the Enemy were within six or Eight miles of my Quarters. I detach'd Col. Lee with a Troop of Dragoons & put the rest of the Light Troops in Motion."[31]

Colonel Lee was actually Lieutenant Colonel Henry Lee of Virginia. He had reinforced Greene in South Carolina with his legion of cavalry and infantry in December, and had arrived with the reputation of a daring (and, some would argue, reckless) commander. Lee's accomplishments at Valley Forge and Paulus Hook in the northern theater earned him multiple promotions and command of a legion. They paled, however, next to the accomplishments he was about to achieve in the South— accomplishments that would earn him the moniker "Light Horse" Harry Lee.

Lieutenant Colonel Lee's men were having breakfast when orders arrived to mount, so he sent only one troop of cavalry under Captain James Armstrong southwestward to investigate, and ordered the rest of his legion to follow after they had finished breakfast.[32] Lee accompanied Armstrong, but after a few miles decided that the report of nearby enemy troops was mistaken. He halted and ordered Captain Armstrong to remain with three dragoons and a local Whig who knew the area while Lee led the rest of the troop back to rejoin the legion.[33]

The civilian guide expressed great anxiety at remaining behind on his tired horse, so Lee ordered his young bugler, James Gillies, to exchange horses with the man. He then sent Gillies back to the light infantry camp to update Colonel Williams.[34]

As Lee and his troopers slowly retraced their route back, they heard gunfire in their rear, where they had left Captain Armstrong. Lee posted the dragoons with him off the road in the woods and waited. Within moments Armstrong and his party came charging past, closely pursued by a troop of enemy cavalry under Captain Patrick Miller of Tarleton's Legion. Neither noticed Lieutenant Colonel Lee and his horsemen.

Lee led his party of dragoons in pursuit of Miller, who was unable to catch Armstrong but overtook James Gillies on the worn-out horse. In a matter of moments the young, unarmed bugler was unhorsed and sabered mercilessly. Lee and his party arrived in time to witness the attack, and charged headlong into Miller and his men. Infuriated by what they considered cold-blooded murder, Lee's men decimated the British dragoons, killing eighteen and capturing Captain Miller and a few others.[35] Lieutenant Colonel Lee angrily reprimanded his troopers when they brought back prisoners; he had instructed that no quarter be given in retaliation for what happened to James Gillies.[36] Lee recalled in his memoirs, written in the third person, that

> Miller, being peremptorily charged with the atrocity perpetrated in his view, was told to prepare for death. The captain, with some show of reason, asserted that intelligence being his object, it was his wish and interest to save the soldier; that he had tried to do so; but his dragoons being intoxicated, all his efforts were ineffectual. He added, that in the terrible slaughter [of the Americans at the Waxaws] his humanity was experienced, and had been acknowledged by some of the Americans who escaped death on that bloody day. Lee was somewhat mollified by this rational apology, and was disposed to substitute one of the prisoners; but soon overtaking the speechless, dying youth . . . when able to speak, confirmed his former impressions, he returned with unrelenting sternness to his first decision. Descending a long hill, he repeated his determination to sacrifice Miller in the vale through which they were about to pass; and handing him a pencil desired him to note on paper whatever he might wish to make known to his friends, with an assurance that it should be transmitted to the British general.[37]

Miller was saved by the approach of the main British column, which forced Lee to abandon Miller's execution and rush the prisoners to the rear.

With Cornwallis now on the trail of the American light corps, Williams hastened his march northward. Every mile of road that

Williams drew Cornwallis down provided Greene with more time to reach the Dan River. The danger for the American light troops, however, was that every step also took them further away from the support of Greene's army. By midday Williams decided that he had provided Greene with an adequate head start to the Dan, so he redirected his march towards Irwin's Ferry to join Greene there.[38]

Lee's Legion assumed the responsibilities of the rear guard. At some point in the march Lee diverted his men onto an obscure path along the route taken by the light corps. He hoped to provide his men with a little rest and then use the path to catch up to the light corps. After a short time on this route Lee encountered a generous farmer, who provided forage for Lee's horses and provisions for his men. Lee recorded in his memoirs what happened next.

> The obscurity of the narrow road taken by Lee lulled every suspicion with respect to the enemy; and a few vedettes only were placed at intermediate points, rather to give notice when the British should pass along, than to guard the Legion from surprise. This precaution was most fortunate; for it so happened that Lord Cornwallis, having ascertained that Greene had directed his course to Irwin's Ferry, determined to avail himself of the nearest route to gain the road of his enemy, and took the path which Lee had selected. Our horses were unbridled, with abundance of provender before them; the hospitable farmer had liberally bestowed his meal and bacon. . . . To the surprise and grief of all, the pleasant prospect was instantly marred by the fire of the advanced vedettes—certain signal of the enemy's approach. Before the farm was a creek, which, in consequence of the late incessant rains, could be passed only by a bridge, not more distant from the enemy then from our party. The cavalry being speedily arrayed, moved to support the vedettes; while the infantry were ordered, in full run, to seize and hold the bridge.
>
> The enemy was equally surprised with ourselves at this unexpected meeting; and the light party in front halted, to report and be directed. This pause was sufficient. The bridge was gained, and soon passed by the corps of Lee. The British fol-

lowed. The road over the bridge leading through cultivated fields for a mile, the British army was in full view of the troops of Lee as the latter ascended the eminence, on whose summit they entered the great road to Irwin's Ferry.[39]

Now the race was really on! With General Cornwallis pressing the American light corps, it was crucial that Colonel Williams's men remain vigilant. Cornwallis's advance troops occasionally came within musket shot of the American rear guard (which was mounted), but they were unable to stop the Americans. Williams halted his march only when the British halted theirs. Lee, who spent most of the march with the rear guard, recalled in his memoirs that "the duty, severe in the day, became more so at night; for numerous patrols and strong pickets were necessarily furnished by the light troops, not only for their own safety, but to prevent the enemy from placing himself by a circuitous march, between Williams and Greene. Such a maneuver would have been fatal to the American army; and, to render it impossible, half of the troops were alternately appointed every night to duty: so that each man, during the retreat, was entitled to but six hours repose in forty-eight."[40]

Such hard duty took a toll on the men and horses, yet the American light troops marched on. At one point it appeared that their efforts to screen the main body had failed when the van of the light corps spotted numerous campfires off in the distance. With Cornwallis still pressing their rear, the American light corps worried that they had caught up to Greene. If this were true, then all of their effort and sacrifice to provide Greene with time to escape had been wasted. As they approached the campfires the exhausted light troops resigned themselves to one last doomed engagement against a vastly superior enemy.[41] Lee recalled that "no pen can describe the heart-rendering feelings of our brave and wearied troops. . . . Our dauntless corps were convinced that the crisis had now arrived when its self sacrifice could alone give a chance of escape of the main body. With one voice was announced the noble resolution to turn on the foe, and by dint of desperate courage, so to cripple him as to force a discontinuance of pursuit."[42]

To the great relief of the light troops, however, it was soon discovered that Greene's troops had left the campsite hours earlier, and that local militia had maintained the fires for the benefit of the light corps.[43] Unfortunately for Colonel Williams and his tired men, the close proximity of Cornwallis prevented the American light troops from enjoying the warmth of the campfires. Williams did find the time to write to Greene, however, and express his anxiety about the slow progress of Greene's main body of troops.

> I was exceedingly concern'd to hear . . . that you were yet 25 miles from the ferry. My Dear General at Sun Down the Enemy were only 22 miles from you and may be in motion now or will most probably [be] by 3 o'Clock in the morning. . . . Rely on it, my Dear Sir, it is possible for you to be overtaken before you can cross the Dan even if you had 20 boats. . . . I conclude you march'd as far today as you could and if your Army can make but Eleven miles in a Day you will not be able to pass the ferry in less than two Days more. In less time than that we will be driven in to your Camp or I must risque the Troops I've the Honor to command and in doing so I risque every thing. . . . The Gentlemen of Cavalry assure me their Horses want refreshment exceedingly and our Infantry are so excessively fatigu'd that I'm confident I lose men every Day. We have been all this Day almost in presence of the Enemy but have sustain'd no loss but of Sick and Strollers.[44]

Despite Williams's pessimism, the Americans marched on. Lee recalled,

> About midnight our troops were put in motion, in consequence of the enemy's advance on our pickets, which the British general had been induced to order, from knowing that he was within forty miles of the Dan, and that all his hopes depended on the exertions of the following day. Animated with the prospect of soon terminating their present labors, the light troops resumed their march with alacrity. The roads continued deep and broken, and were rendered worse by being incrusted

with frost: nevertheless, the march was pushed with great expedition.[45]

Cornwallis described his pursuit in similar terms. "Nothing could exceed the patience and alacrity of the officers and soldiers under every species of hardship and fatigue, in endeavouring to overtake [the Americans]: But our intelligence upon this occasion was exceedingly defective; which, with heavy rains, bad roads, and the passage of many deep creeks, and bridges destroyed by the enemy's light troops, rendered all our exertions vain."[46]

Good news finally reached the American light troops on February 14, in a series of messages from Greene informing Williams of the army's arrival at the Dan River. Greene wrote at 2 P.M. that "the greater part of our wagons are over and the troops are crossing," and at 5:30 P.M. Greene announced: "The stage is clear."[47]

The news inspired the light troops to march with renewed vigor, and they reached the ferry crossings hours ahead of the British. Greene greeted Williams at the riverbank and crossed to the north side with him. Lee arrived with his legion soon after and proudly recalled in his memoirs that he was the last to cross the Dan River.[48] The American army had achieved its goal; it had crossed the Dan River intact.

Cornwallis ended his pursuit at the Dan River. Just 150 miles to the east were 1,800 troops under Benedict Arnold in Portsmouth, but Cornwallis remained focused on securing North Carolina and bringing Greene to battle. Cornwallis withdrew south, to Hillsborough, to rest his tired army and rally Tory support in North Carolina.

Arnold, who followed up his very successful raid up the James River in January with the occupation of Portsmouth in southeastern Virginia, also sought to attract Tory support. Since their arrival in Portsmouth on January 20, Arnold's 1,800 men had kept busy constructing earthworks and redoubts along the land approaches (mostly on the western edge of town). The small fleet of warships and transports that had conveyed Arnold's expedition to Virginia defended the water approach to Portsmouth along the Elizabeth River. While his men dug in, Arnold awaited word from Cornwallis, unaware that Daniel Morgan's victory at Cowpens had once again disrupted Cornwallis's plans for North Carolina. Just a few miles to the west of Portsmouth, hundreds of Virginia militia sat, eager but unready to strike at Arnold and his men.

BY VIRTUE OF HIS Continental commission General Frederick von Steuben commanded Virginia's military forces in the winter of 1781. Disappointed by the slow initial response of the militia to Arnold's invasion, Steuben found himself in a much better position by the end of January. Thousands of militia were in the field and deployed on both sides of the James River, but despite their large numbers a severe shortage of arms and equipment—particularly tents, kettles, and axes—limited their effectiveness. The makeshift camps of the militia provided many of the men with inadequate shelter, and they grew sick from prolonged exposure to the elements. General Robert Lawson, a veteran of the Continental army in command of militia troops at Mackie's Mill, reported to Governor Jefferson on January 28.

> We have no Tents; and are posted where we cannot have the benefit of Houses. The severity of the Season coming on daily, the Baron ordered us to build Hutts; but this cannot be done without proper Tools, and those we have not as yet been able to procure. . . . Indeed it is a lamentable fact that we have [not enough axes] for the purpose of cutting wood to make fires for the Men, who are decreasing my strength daily by sickness, occasion'd I am confident from their expos'd state to the severity of the excessive bad weather we have had in this quarter. We want exceedingly ammunition Waggons, with proper military Chests, Cartridges, and almost every article of Camp Equipment.[49]

General Peter Muhlenberg, another veteran of the Continental army and former brigade commander of Continental troops, assumed field command of the militia south of the James River when General Steuben returned to Richmond in late January. He described a similar situation for his eight hundred troops at Cabin Point: "General Lawson complains heavily of the wretched situation of the sick in his camp, who are without medicine, physicians, and necessaries.

We are here [at Cabin Point] in the same situation, and no other alternative is left us than to disperse the sick in the neighboring houses."[50]

The shortage of supplies, particularly arms, was an important factor behind the decision of Steuben and his subordinate officers to forego an assault on Portsmouth and instead attempt only to confine Arnold's movements to the vicinity of Portsmouth. Militia detachments were posted outside of Portsmouth accordingly. Hundreds of other militia troops were posted across the James River at Williamsburg.

VIRGINIA'S FORCES were not the only ones scattered; Arnold established two key British outposts a few miles south and east of Portsmouth, in Norfolk and Princess Anne County, to help secure forage and provisions for his troops and defend the approaches to Portsmouth. Approximately one hundred troops with two cannon were posted in a strong redoubt at the village of Great Bridge. Captain Johann Ewald, who accompanied this detachment to Great Bridge described the location in his diary: "Great Bridge is an important position in Virginia if Portsmouth is to be designated and maintained as a fortified post. It consists of a village of twenty-five fine buildings and is inhabited by tradespeople, who had . . . all flown [away]."[51]

Ewald noted that several small creeks flowed into the southern branch of the Elizabeth River at Great Bridge and created "an impenetrable marsh of fifteen or sixteen hundred paces."[52] The marsh was overcome by "a single causeway [which] passes over this swampland, and there is a wooden bridge in the middle which rests on trestles and piers."[53] The wooden bridge was over two hundred paces in length and was the primary crossing point for nearly all travelers to and from northeastern North Carolina and southeastern Virginia. Thus, control of the Great Bridge was essential for the security of Arnold and his men in Portsmouth.

The other important outpost that Arnold fortified outside of Portsmouth was a few miles to the northeast of Great Bridge. Three roads converged on the village of Kemp's Landing, which was located at the headwater of the eastern branch of the Elizabeth River. From Kemp's Landing, one could travel straight to Norfolk, just seven miles to the west; Norfolk, which lay in ruins after it was burned in 1776, lay directly across the Elizabeth River from Portsmouth and Arnold's troops. The village of Kemp's Landing was three times the size of Great Bridge, yet the British garrison left to defend this important intersection in Princess Anne County numbered only sixty men, just over half of the force guarding the Great Bridge.[54]

Arnold undoubtedly would have preferred to leave more troops at these outposts, but with so many men needed to build and defend the lines on the western edge of Portsmouth he had few to spare, especially since he sent regular patrols into the countryside to reconnoiter and forage. One such foraging party was ambushed in late January on the road to Great Bridge. Ewald observed that the culprits were "said to have been from a light corps commanded by a certain Major Weeks, to whom the country people are greatly devoted, partly from inclination and partly from fear. In the countryside he is considered an excellent officer and a good partisan. There was much talk about him at Kemp's Landing, but we laughed because we had neither seen nor heard anyone. Afterward, we were astonished over the trick [ambush] that he had played in our rear."[55]

Major Amos Weeks was an experienced militia commander who had led Princess Anne County troops since the beginning of the war. For a brief period in February 1781, Major Weeks represented the only active opposition to General Arnold in Portsmouth. His troops staged a series of daring ambushes and raids throughout Princess Anne County upon both Arnold's troops and the loyalists who looked to Arnold for protection. The actions of Weeks eventually prompted Arnold to send two strong detachments under Ewald and Lieutenant Colonel Simcoe to subdue the aggressive militia commander. Ewald recalled that on February 12 "the news came in from Princess Anne County that Major Weeks was spreading ruin in the area and severely harassing the few good loyalists. The communication between Portsmouth and Great Bridge was made unsafe. Therefore, Arnold decided to send two parties there, one under Simcoe and the other under myself, in order to drive away the honorable gentleman."[56]

Simcoe commanded two hundred infantry and forty cavalry, and Ewald the same number with ten fewer cavalry. Simcoe headed for Kemp's Landing while Ewald marched to Great Bridge. The plan called for Simcoe to occupy Major Weeks's attention by marching straight at his reported location east of Kemp's Landing, while Ewald circled around to the rear of the militia by crossing Devil's Elbow Swamp (which lay between Great Bridge and Kemp's Landing) to strike Weeks from behind. Ewald recorded in his diary that

> I departed at once from the vicinity of Great Bridge, crossed the Devil's Elbow Swamp—two good hours wide—and about nine o'clock in the morning arrived on the other side at a plantation which belonged to a loyalist and a relative of my guide. This swampy wood was crossed on a very dark night. . . . The men had to march in single file, constantly going up to their knees in the swamp. We had to climb over countless trees which the wind had blown down and that often lay crosswise, over which the horses could scarcely go. They had to be whistled at continually to prevent them from going astray. Men and horses were so worn out that they could hardly go on when I happily left this abominable region behind.[57]

A coded message from Simcoe instructing Ewald to continue on through Dauge's swamp awaited Ewald at the plantation. The German captain obediently led his detachment onward and recalled,

> Although I had crossed the first swamp with great difficulty during the night, this last passage surpassed the first one very much with respect to all hardships. The men had to wade constantly over their knees in the swampy water and climb over the most dangerous spots with the help of fallen and rotted trees. At times there were places such that if a foothold were missed, a man could have suffocated in the swamp. I had to cross a flooded, swampy cypress wood with the cavalry, a quarter of an hour further to the right, where one had to ride continually in water over the saddle. At the end of the swamp, wither our two guides led us safely at the same time, there was

a log causeway—a good quarter hour long—which because of its great holes was just as difficult for the horses and men to cross as the swamp had been.[58]

Ewald and his men surprised the occupants of a small house and learned from them that Major Weeks had just burned Dauge's Bridge, southeast of Kemp's Landing, and withdrawn. Through a combination of persuasion (in the form of monetary reward) and threat (to hang the occupants if they didn't cooperate), Ewald learned that Weeks was seen just a few hours earlier with six to eight hundred troops at a nearby plantation. (The actual number of militia with Weeks was 520.)[59] Despite being significantly outnumbered, Ewald was determined to attack. He sent Captain Shank with the cavalry (thirty strong) and twenty jaegers straight down the road to the plantation where Weeks was reportedly encamped to open the attack while Ewald circled through the woods with the rest of his detachment (180 strong) to strike the rebels on their flank. "I had marched scarcely eight hundred to a thousand paces when I heard strong rifle fire," Ewald recalled.[60] His guide speculated that Weeks was actually camped at a closer plantation, so Ewald had to adjust his attack on the fly:

> I quickly formed a front on the flank and directed my men to fire a volley as soon as they caught sight of the enemy and then boldly attack the foe with the bayonet and hunting sword. I ordered the jagers to disperse on both flanks and kept the rangers in close formation. We had not passed five to six hundred paces through the wood when we saw the enemy in a line facing the side of the highway to London Bridge, firing freely against Captain Shank's advance. In doing so, they carelessly showed us their left flank. I got over a fence safely without being discovered by the enemy. Here I had a volley fired, blew the half-moon, and shouted, 'Hurrah!' I scrambled over a second fence and threw myself at the enemy, who was so surprised that he impulsively fled in the greatest disorder into the wood lying behind him. At this moment the gallant Captain Shank advanced with his cavalry, ably supported by Lieutenant

[Alexander] Bickell with his twenty jagers. Some sixty men were either cut down or bayoneted by the infantry. We captured one captain, one lieutenant, four noncommissioned officers, and forty-five men, some sound and some wounded. All the baggage, along with a powder cart and a wagon loaded with weapons, was taken as booty by the men. I ordered Lieutenant Bickell with all the foot jagers to quickly follow the enemy into the wood. He followed him until night fell and brought back seven more prisoners. On my side, I had three jagers and two rangers wounded and one horse killed.[61]

Ewald's efforts had resulted in a decisive victory, and he sent word of the engagement to Simcoe, who was a few miles north of Ewald at London Bridge. Ewald and his detachment rested at James's plantation until the morning, during which Ewald attempted to convince some of the militia prisoners to join the Crown side. "I learned from the prisoners that Major Weeks designated daily a rallying point where they were to reassemble after a reverse. He seldom remained in one place for twenty-four hours, and toward evening they were on the march again. Their present rendezvous was Northwest Landing. The enemy strength had been 520 men, and his people were so devoted to him that none of them were willing to enlist in our service."[62]

Simcoe and his detachment joined Ewald in the morning, and both detachments marched southward to Pungo Church on the assumption that Weeks would pass there on his way to Northwest Landing. Simcoe and Ewald reached the church before noon, searched the area, and set up an ambush. Simcoe then took his cavalry to a nearby plantation and suggested that Ewald march to another plantation east of Pungo with the rest of his detachment. On his march there, one of Ewald's men spotted "several sentries in blue coats at a distance of several hundred yards."[63] Worried that the enemy had discovered him, Ewald divided his jaegers into two groups and ordered them off the road to approach the plantation from the right and left. Ewald led the rangers that were with him straight up the road towards the plantation. Fighting erupted to the right of the road, and Ewald's detachments converged on the sound of battle. He recalled,

I found the enemy in full flight, running through a marshy meadow to a wood. Two of their men were killed and a lieutenant with five men captured. Had Lieutenant Bickell seized another officer who stood a few paces away instead of the lieutenant, the commander of the party—Major Weeks himself—would have been captured. But since he was not as well dressed as the lieutenant, he was not taken for an officer. Just before, a jager had killed his horse. This man, whom I had the good luck to chase all around, knew the countryside better than I could ever know it. That was evident from the positions he took, for a retreat always remained open to him in the impassable woods which he alone knew. But on this occasion, my spies were better than his; and luck, on which everything depends in war, was on my side.[64]

ALTHOUGH THE EFFORTS of Ewald and Simcoe handed Weeks a series of defeats in mid-February, the Virginians managed to score a small victory of their own on the outskirts of Portsmouth. On February 17, General Muhlenberg, encouraged by the arrival of three powerful French warships, decided to increase the pressure on Arnold in Portsmouth by marching 1,100 troops to within a mile and a half of Arnold's lines. Muhlenberg recounted to General Greene that "I marched . . . with six hundred riflemen and five hundred musketry, with which we formed an ambuscade about one mile and a half from Portsmouth and on the morning of the 18th, a party of horse was ordered to charge the [enemy] picket, which was posted within shot of their redoubts. The horse charged and took the picket, consisting of a sergeant, corporal, and twelve men without having a shot fired at them."[65]

General Muhlenberg added that two jaegers and three pioneers were killed in the charge, and a wagon and six horses were seized. Muhlenberg apparently had more in mind than just capturing some of the enemy's sentinels posted along a picket line, for a Virginia soldier who participated in the engagement recalled that:

a detachment of horse was sent forward to skirmish with the pickets of the enemy. . . . They were ordered to retreat in haste and draw the enemy on to Hall's Mill dam, they were then to wheel and attack in front while the Militia took them in flank and rear. It was hoped that they might easily be taken. The Militia passed the night under arms. It was a dreadful night, thundering and lightening, though in the depths of winter and clearing off so piercingly cold that the ponds were covered with ice before morning. The enemy did not follow.[66]

Had Muhlenberg realized at the time that Arnold only had three hundred effective troops to man the lines in Portsmouth—the rest of his army being sick, away from Portsmouth on the hunt for Major Weeks, or posted at Great Bridge and Kemp's Landing—he might have risked a direct assault on Arnold's lines.[67] Alas, the opportunity passed, and the departure of the French ships on February 19 (surprisingly, after a successful engagement with Arnold's fleet in which they captured the HMS *Romulus* and two privateers), coupled with the return of Simcoe and Ewald (with nearly five hundred men), secured Portsmouth for the time being.

A few days after this close call for Arnold, he met with over four hundred inhabitants of Princess Anne County at Kemp's Landing to administer an oath of allegiance to England and convince the loyal Virginians to become more involved in suppressing the American rebellion.[68] Captain Ewald observed the meeting and bitterly noted that those present "gladly swallowed the oath," after assurances were given of their protection, but few stepped forward to join the fight against the rebels. Ewald actually challenged a wealthy loyalist, "one of the most distinguished and richest residents of this area," to raise a battalion of troops for the defense of Princess Anne County.[69] The gentleman explained to Ewald that he had to first be certain that the British would honor their pledge to stay. "You have already been in this area twice. General Leslie gave me the same assurances in the past autumn, and where is he now?" asked the loyal Virginian.[70] Ewald was disgusted by this comment, and exclaimed: "How can you be called friends of the King if you won't venture anything for the right cause? Look at your Opposition Party [the American rebels]: they abandon wife, child, house, and home, and let us lay waste to everything. They fight without shoes and clothing with all passion, suffer hunger, and gladly endure all hardships of war. But you loyalists won't do anything! You only want to be protected, to live in peace in your houses. We are supposed to break our bones for you, in place of yours, to accomplish your purpose. We attempt everything, and sacrifice our own blood for your assumed cause."[71]

Later, after he had calmed down and returned to Portsmouth with Arnold, Ewald realized that "this man, who did not want to be a soldier, would have been a fool if he had acted as I had advised him. For he possessed a fortune in property . . . and had for a wife one of the most charming blondes that I have ever seen in all my life!"[72]

Luckily for Arnold, his inability to attract greater loyalist support did not lead to any military reverses on the field against the numerically superior rebels. In fact, the remainder of February saw little activity between the two sides. Muhlenberg revealed the main reason for his restrained actions in a letter to General Greene on February 24:

> I must acknowledge it is derogatory to the honour of the state to suffer such a handful of men [under Arnold] to retain possession [of Portsmouth for] so long; but what . . . is to be done? They are strongly fortified; I have near two thousand men, but among the whole about three hundred bayonets and two brass six pound [cannon]. With such a military apparatus, we cannot think of attacking the works by regular approaches, and all my hopes at present are, that I shall be able to coop up Arnold so close that he will be obliged to make an attempt to dislodge us.[73]

ONE HUNDRED AND FIFTY MILES to the west of Portsmouth, General Nathanael Greene would have welcomed the opportunity to "coop up" Cornwallis, or at least turn and face him in battle, but his desperately needed reinforcements from Virginia were not waiting for Greene on the north bank of the Dan River, so he retreated ten miles further north to Halifax Courthouse and hoped that Cornwallis would not pursue. Greene pessimistically updated Governor Jefferson on his situation on February 15, the day after he crossed the river:

> Our Army is so great an object with Lord Cornwallis, and the reduction of the Southern States depend so much upon it, that I think it highly probable he will push us still farther; and I am not without my apprehensions that he will oblige us to risqué a general action, however contrary to our wishes or interest, which cannot fail to prove ruinous to the Army as our force is but little more than one half the enemy's, and there are few or no Militia that have joined us on our March, or at least not more than one or two hundred. . . . Unless our Army is greatly reinforced I see nothing to prevent [the enemy's] future progress.[74]

Greene gave an equally bleak assessment of his situation to General Washington.

> Lord Cornwallis has been at our heels from day to day ever since we left Guilford and our movements from thence to this place have been of the most critical kind, having a river in our front, and the enemy in our rear. But happily we have crossed without the loss of either men or Stores. . . . The enemy are on the other side of the [Dan] river and as it is falling, I expect it will be fordable before night; and the fords are so numerous, and the enemy lay in such an advantageous situation for crossing that it would be a folly to think of defending them, as it would reduce our force to small parties which might prove our ruin. The miserable situation of the troops for want of clothing has rendered the march the most painful imaginable, several hundreds of the Soldiers tracking the ground with their bloody feet. . . . The enemy's movements have been so rapid and the Country under such terror that few or no Militia have joined us, and the greater part we had have fallen off. . . . Nothing is yet done to give me effectual support and I am not a little apprehensive that it is out of the power of Virginia & North Carolina to afford it.[75]

Greene's apprehension eased somewhat the next day, however, when reports informed him that Cornwallis intended to march south to Hillsborough, North Carolina. Greene was further encouraged by the arrival of long-awaited Virginia militia reinforcements and reports of even larger numbers of militia on the march to join the army. Just two days after his pessimistic letters to Jefferson and Washington, Greene, confident that his newly reinforced army could now stand against Cornwallis, tried to tempt the British commander into actually crossing the Dan River. Greene reported that "our Army is on the North side of the Banister River, encamped at Halifax Courthouse in Virginia, in order to tempt the Enemy to cross the [Dan] River, as the most pleasing prospect presents itself of a strong reinforcement from the Militia of this State."[76]

When it became clear that Cornwallis would not cross the Dan River to continue his pursuit of Greene, the American commander ordered General Andrew Pickens, who was still in North Carolina with approximately seven hundred militia troops, to harass and delay Cornwallis on his march south to Hillsborough.[77] Greene hoped to turn the tables on Cornwallis, recross the Dan River, and attack Cornwallis with his reinforced army.

Four

Cornwallis Catches Greene

MARCH 1781

L IEUTENANT COLONEL HENRY LEE AND HIS LEGION RECROSSED
the Dan River ahead of General Greene's army to pursue their
former pursuers on February 18. Two days later, Lee informed Greene
that he was only twenty-five miles from Hillsborough and that advanced parties of his horsemen had reached the enemy's lines.[1] The
next day Greene, who was still at the Dan River with the rest of his
reinforced army, confidently wrote to General Pickens that "if we can
get up with the enemy, I have no doubt of giving a good account of
them."[2] Greene's enthusiasm to attack Cornwallis cooled considerably
the following day (February 22), however, when he learned that a
large reinforcement of riflemen he had expected to join him did not
actually exist. Greene halted his march south in response to this disappointing news, and instead ordered his advance detachments under
Pickens, Lieutenant Colonel Lee, and Colonel Otho Williams (with
the light corps) to watch for opportunities to harass the British and
their Tory supporters.

Lee and Pickens joined forces outside Hillsborough on February 23, and learned two days later that a British detachment under Banastre Tarleton of 200 cavalry, 150 British infantry, and 100 German jaegers was nearby. Tarleton had been sent out from Hillsborough to protect a detachment of Tory militia that had formed under Colonel John Pyle.[3] Lee and Pickens immediately set out to attack Tarleton. When Lee encountered a small patrol of Colonel Pyle's mounted Tories, he deceived them into believing that he was Tarleton with the British Legion. This bold deception was possible because Lee and his men, who had advanced ahead of Pickens's militia, were dressed remarkably like Tarleton's force—namely, in short green coats and leather caps.[4] The Tory scouts returned to Pyle with a request from Lee (acting as Tarleton) to clear the road for "Tarleton's" detachment. Lee claimed in his memoirs that, since Tarleton was his primary objective, he planned to avoid a fight with Pyle's Tories. Instead, he intended to "make known to [Colonel Pyle] his real character as soon as he should confront him, with a solemn assurance of his and his associates perfect exemption from injury, and with the choice of returning to their homes, or of taking a more generous part, by uniting with the defenders of their common country against a common foe."[5]

As it turned out, Lee was unable to offer either of these options to Pyle. Instead, a bloody one-sided fight erupted. Lee recalled the incident in his memoirs.

Lee passed along the line at the head of the column with a smiling countenance, dropping, occasionally, expressions complimentary to the good looks and commendable conduct of his loyal friends. At length he reached Colonel Pyle, when the customary civilities were promptly interchanged. Grasping Pyle by the hand, Lee was in the act of consummating his plan, when the enemy's left, discovering Pickens's militia, not sufficiently concealed, began to fire upon the rear of the cavalry commanded by Captain Eggleston. This officer instantly turned upon the foe, as did immediately the whole column. This conflict was quickly decided, and bloody on one side only.[6]

Captain Joseph Graham, the commander of a company of mounted North Carolina militia, attributed the engagement to a different cause. He recalled that he and his men initially believed Pyle's men to be comrades, but soon realized their mistake.

> I riding in front of the Militia dragoons, near to Capt. Eggleston who brought up Lee's rear, at a distance of forty or fifty yards, pointed out to him, the strip of red cloth on the hats of Pyle's men, as the mark of Tories. Eggleston appeared to doubt this, until he came nearly opposite to the end of their line, when riding up to the man on their left, who appeared as an officer, he inquired, "Who do you belong to?" The answer was promptly given, "To King George," upon which Eggleston struck him on the head with his sword. Our [militia] dragoons well knew the red cloth on the hats to be the badge of Tories, but being under the immediate command of Lee, they had waited for orders. But seeing the example set by this officer, without waiting for further commands, they rushed upon them like a torrent. Lee's men, next to the [front] discovering this, reined in their horses to the right upon the Tory line, and in less than one minute the engagement was general.[7]

At the loss of not a single man, Lee and Pickens destroyed Colonel Pyle's detachment. Estimates of Tory casualties vary, but it is clear that approximately one hundred were killed and an equal number were wounded—many grievously, by the legion's sabers. One important factor in the lopsided outcome was the continued belief among many of Pyle's men (even as they were being cut down) that Lee's Legion was actually Tarleton's Legion. Instead of fighting back, many Tories exclaimed their support for the king, thinking that this would halt the attack. Instead, they were struck down.[8]

Although the engagement was a decisive and victorious affair for the Americans, it was a fight that Lee had wished to avoid. Lee confirmed this in a letter to Greene on the evening of the engagement: "The Legion cavalry passed [Pyle's men] agreeable to order, as if British troops. I did this, that no time might be lost in reaching Col Tarleton. The enemy discovered their mistake on the near approach of our militia & commenced action."[9]

General Pickens, who was near the rear of the American force, also viewed the incident negatively and considered it a missed opportunity to surprise Tarleton.

> Never was there a more glorious opportunity of cutting off a detachment [Tarleton's] than this when . . . our sanguine expectations were blasted by our falling in with a body of from two to three hundred Tories, under the command of a Colonel Piles . . . they suffered Colonel Lee's Horse to pass equal with their front. Our men were in some measure under the same mistake [unaware that Pyle's men were the enemy] but soon found out, and nigh one hundred were killed and the greatest part of the others wounded.[10]

Although this one-sided affair cost Lee and Pickens a chance to surprise Banastre Tarleton, the brutality of the fight and its outcome had a chilling effect on future Tory support for the British in North Carolina. Furthermore, Lee and Pickens had not given up on attacking Tarleton. Reinforced at the end of the day by hundreds of newly arrived Virginia riflemen under Colonel William Preston, Lee's men spent the night within a few miles of Tarleton. They hoped to engage Tarleton at daybreak, but the British commander stole an early morning march on the Americans and returned to Hillsborough unscathed.

Cornwallis and his reunited army of over two thousand men departed Hillsborough the same day, and marched west to obtain more plentiful provisions and protect the king's friends (Tories) between the Haw and Deep Rivers.[11]

Greene, who was north of the Haw River with the main body of the American army, responded cautiously to Cornwallis's movements. He led his troops southward and linked up with Lee and Pickens.[12] Greene pushed the army across the Haw River the next day, and sent the light corps under Colonel Williams farther south across Reedy Fork Creek to screen the army and locate the enemy. Williams, in turn, sent Lee and his legion, as well as a detachment of Colonel Preston's riflemen and parties of North Carolina militia, even farther south to patrol along Alamance Creek.[13] On March 2, Lee's detachment engaged a large enemy party in a brief but heated skirmish. A much larger engagement involving the entire American light corps erupted four days later at Weitzel's Mill along Reedy Fork Creek.

The engagement at Weitzel's Mill was prompted by Cornwallis's attempt to catch the American light corps by surprise. On the evening of March 5, Cornwallis was informed that Williams's light corps "was posted carelessly at separate plantations for the convenience of [foraging]."[14] Cornwallis marched his army towards the American light troops early the next morning, hoping to "drive them in and . . . attack General Greene's [main body] if an opportunity offered."[15] Greene had moved his troops back across the Haw River and was relatively safe, but Williams and his light troops were much closer to Cornwallis and unaware of the threat. Fortunately for the Americans, Cornwallis's movement was detected by an American patrol. Williams recalled, "[The enemy] had approach'd within two miles of our position, and their intention was manifestly to surprise us. I immediately order'd the Troops to march to [Weitzel's] Mill and soon after was inform'd by two Prisoners that the Enemy were marching for the same place on a road parallel to that in which we were."[16]

As the Americans and British raced to Weitzel's Mill to cross Reedy Fork Creek, Williams ordered Lee's Legion, Lieutenant Colonel William Washington's cavalry, and Virginia riflemen under Colonel William Campbell and Colonel William Preston to slow the enemy's march. Williams reported that "we annoy'd them by Light flanking parties and moved on briskly to the Mill, but were so closely press'd by Col [James] Webster's Brigade & Lt Col Tarltons Legion that I found it absolutely necessary to leave a covering party under the Command of Col [William] Preston."[17]

When they reached the creek, Colonel Preston's riflemen were ordered to hold their position and screen the rest of the light corps as they crossed. Captain Joseph Graham, with a company of mounted North Carolina militia, witnessed this and recalled: "[Colonel Williams] stationed two companies of riflemen, behind trees, one on each side of the road. Thirty poles behind these, as the ground began to turn, he formed a line of militia facing the enemy."[18]

While the bulk of the American light troops safely crossed Reedy Fork Creek and formed on a ridge overlooking the north bank,

Colonel Preston struggled to hold back the British advance guard with his riflemen. Captain Graham described Preston's brief stand:

> The day was still cloudy, a light rain falling at times; the air was calm and dense. The riflemen kept up a severe fire, retreating from tree to tree to the flanks of our second [militia] line. When the enemy approached this, a brisk fire commenced on both sides. . . . They became enveloped in smoke; the fire had lasted but a short time, when the militia were seen running down the hill from under the smoke. The ford was crowded, many passing the watercourse at other places. Some, it was said, were drowned.[19]

Preston's men fought well, but suffered for their stubbornness. Cornwallis bragged later that "the back mountain men and some militia suffered considerably, with little loss on our side."[20] Banastre Tarleton estimated American losses at Weitzel's Mill to be upwards of a hundred killed, wounded, or captured versus only thirty British casualties.[21] American accounts of their losses were much lower. Williams reported to Greene that upwards of twenty-five militia were killed or wounded at Weitzel's Mill as well as a handful of Continentals.[22]

With the entire British army bearing down on the ford, Williams was anxious to withdraw his light corps toward Greene. Williams recalled, "I waited only 'till Col. Preston cross'd and then order'd the Troops to retire. The Enemy pursued some distance but receiving several severe checks from small covering parties and being cow'd by our Cavalry [Cornwallis] thought proper to Halt. We continued to retire about five mile."[23]

Although the American light corps had performed admirably and casualties were relatively light, significant resentment existed among Colonel Preston's militia riflemen about how they were used in the battle. Many felt they had been inappropriately endangered and sacrificed at Weitzel's Mill to protect the Continental light troops, and as soon as they got the chance many of the riflemen left the army for home.[24] One Virginia officer reported the dissention among the militia to Governor Jefferson a few days after the battle: "On the late Skirmish . . . the Riflemen complained that the burden, and heat, of the Day was entirely thrown upon them, and that they were to be made a sacrifice by the Regular Officers to screen their own Troops. Some [of the militia] rejoin'd their Regiments with the main Body and others thought it a plausible excuse for their return home."[25]

The disgruntlement and departure of the militia temporarily weakened Greene's army, and may have influenced his decision to dissolve the light corps and form two smaller corps of observation under Lieutenant Colonels Lee and Washington. Greene informed Lee of the new arrangement in a letter on March 9.

> The light Infantry is dissolvd, and the Army will take upon itself an entire new formation. Col Williams will join the line. And I propose in lieu of the light Infantry two parties of observation, one to be commanded by you, and the other by Lt Col Washington. You are to attend to the enemies movements upon the left wing and Washington upon the right. It is my intention to give Col Washington about 70 or 80 Infantry and between three & four hundred riffleman to act with him. Col Campbell I mean shall join you with about the same number of riflemen, and you and Col Washington either separately or conjunctively as you may agree, to give the enemy all the annoyance in your power, and each to report to Head Quarters.[26]

Greene confessed that he was uncertain of Cornwallis's intentions and instructed Lee to "observe his motions with great attention and give me the earliest information."[27] Greene also expressed his frustration with the militia, but declared that he still planned to pursue Cornwallis once reliable reinforcements arrived. "I am vexed to my soul with the Militia, they desert us by hundreds nay by thousands. I am now waiting for Gen Caswell [with North Carolina militia] reinforcements and the Continental troops [from Virginia] to join us. . . . After which we shall march in pursuit of the enemy as soon as possible, tho our force will not be very respectable."[28]

Lee informed Greene two days later that Cornwallis had moved to the vicinity of Guilford Courthouse, nearly twenty miles southwest of the American army, and urged the American commander to confront Cornwallis.[29]

Lee followed his own advice and posted his detachment close to the British. He also maintained constant patrols to guard against a sudden movement by Cornwallis.[30] While Greene waited along the Haw River for reinforcements to arrive, Cornwallis marched his army a few miles southwest of Guilford Courthouse. He still hoped to attract Tory support and engage Greene, but his supply situation was dire so he also made plans to march southeast towards Cross Creek (modern-day Fayetteville) to resupply and refresh his famished men.[31] These plans were temporarily set aside when Cornwallis learned that Greene and his army were on the march to Guilford Courthouse.

As Greene had hoped, the arrival of long-awaited reinforcements— including 400 Virginia Continentals, 1,000 North Carolina militia, and 1,200 Virginia militia—significantly bolstered Greene's force. As a result, Greene's army surpassed four thousand men, and he decided to act on Lee's advice. He explained his decision to confront Cornwallis in a letter to Congress on March 16. "Finding that our force was much more respectable than it had been, and that there was a much greater probability of its declining than increasing, and that there would be the greatest difficulty in subsisting it long in the field in this exhausted Country, I took the resolution of attacking the Enemy."[32]

GREENE'S ARMY of 4,400 men bivouacked at Guilford Courthouse on March 14, 1781, with plans to attack Cornwallis the next day.[33] As a precaution against a sudden enemy advance, Greene posted Lieutenant Colonel Washington with part of his corps of observation upon the main road to Salisbury. Lee and his legion were posted three miles west of Guilford Courthouse along the New Garden Road to guard against a surprise from that direction. They were joined by a portion of Colonel William Campbell's riflemen (approximately sixty) and a company of Virginia Continental infantry.[34] Lee sent a few of his dragoons under Lieutenant James Heard farther west to patrol the outskirts of the British camp.

Early in the morning of March 15, Lieutenant Heard reported that the enemy was on the move. Lee informed Greene, and led his

detachment toward the British camp to investigate further. Lee's infantry and riflemen were unable to keep pace with his dragoons, so
they trailed behind at a jog.

Off in the distance, a ragged volley echoed through the early
morning, followed shortly after by the appearance of Lieutenant
Heard and his detachment. Heard confirmed to Lee that the British
army was advancing and that their vanguard, commanded by Banastre Tarleton, was right behind him. Lee ordered his dragoons to retire
eastward toward his infantry. As they did so, Tarleton's force caught
up to Lee and attacked. The engagement occurred near a section of
road bordered by steep banks and high fences, which limited each
side's maneuverability. Confident in the superiority of his cavalry,
Lee initially withdrew down the road, but suddenly swung his dragoons around and charged toward the oncoming enemy. He described the outcome of this bold move in his memoirs.

> The charge was ordered by Lee, from conviction that he
> should trample his enemy under foot, if he dared to meet the
> shock; and thus gain an easy and complete victory. But only the
> front section of each corps closed, Tarleton sounding a retreat,
> the moment he discovered [Lee's] column in charge. The whole
> of the enemy's section was dismounted, and many of the horses
> prostrated; some of the dragoons killed, the rest made prisoners;
> not a single American soldier or horse [was] injured.[35]

Lee and his dragoons pursued Tarleton westward toward New
Garden Meeting House, where they ran into a detachment of troops
from the main British army. A volley from the British infantry dismounted a number of Lee's dragoons, including Lee himself. He escaped by taking the mount of one of his troopers, who instantly
offered his horse to Lee. The rattled legion commander then ordered
his dragoons to retreat.[36] As Lee's cavalry withdrew, his legion infantry and Colonel Campbell's riflemen, no doubt tired and footsore,
arrived upon the scene and entered the fray. Lee recalled that "while
the cavalry were retiring, the Legion infantry came running up with
trailed arms, and opened a well-aimed fire upon the guards, which
was followed in a few minutes by a volley from the riflemen under

Colonel Campbell, who had taken post on the left of the infantry. The action became very sharp, and was bravely maintained on both sides."[37]

Concerned that Cornwallis and the entire British army would arrive at any moment, Lee conducted a successful fighting withdrawal eastward toward Guilford Courthouse.

Four miles to the east, Greene and the rest of the American army heard Lee's engagement and prepared to meet the enemy. Greene borrowed the tactics of General Daniel Morgan at Cowpens and divided his force into separate lines. Over a thousand North Carolina militia held the first line, which bordered woods and extended along a fence. To their front were open fields, over which the British had to march. General Greene asked the militia in the first line to fire two good volleys at the British before they retreated to the rear.[38] To anchor this line, Greene placed Lieutenant Colonel Washington's detachment on the right flank and Lee's force (upon their arrival from the New Garden Meetinghouse fight) on the left. Two six-pound cannon were posted in the road, which bisected the militia line down the middle.

Greene formed a second line of militia about three hundred yards behind the first. These troops, numbering about 1,200, were Virginians under General Robert Lawson and General Edward Stevens. They used the wooded terrain around them for protection and braced themselves for the fight.

General Stevens was particularly anxious for his men to redeem Virginia's honor after the appalling conduct of the state militia at Camden seven months earlier. Hundreds of Virginians had fled the Camden battlefield without firing a shot, and Stevens was determined to prevent a repeat of that humiliation. To ensure that his men held their ground, Stevens posted a number of sentinels twenty yards behind the line with instructions to shoot the first man who retreated without orders.[39]

The third and last American line was posted on a hill adjacent to the road near the courthouse, approximately eight hundred yards behind the Virginia militia. Fourteen hundred Continentals from Maryland, Delaware, and Virginia held this position.[40] Most of the Virginia Continentals were newly raised recruits with little military experience. They were placed on the right of the line and commanded by General Isaac Huger. Colonel Otho Williams commanded the more seasoned Maryland troops on the left.

The Battle of Guilford Courthouse commenced around noon when elements of Cornwallis's army crossed Little Horsepen Creek, eight hundred yards in front of Greene's first line.[41] Greene's artillery opened fire on the British, who responded with their own cannon fire. While the artillery crews blasted away, Cornwallis crossed the creek with the rest of his army and deployed his troops along a thousand-yard front.[42]

Around 1 P.M., approximately two thousand British and German soldiers advanced over open ground toward Greene's first line. The North Carolinians anxiously waited for the enemy to advance within range of their smoothbore muskets, preferably a hundred yards or less. The tension proved unbearable, and a ragged volley was unleashed by a portion of the militia at 140 yards.[43]

The British continued their advance, sparking panic in the center of the North Carolina line. Some of the militia dropped their gear and fled to the rear. The troops on the flanks held, however, and leveled their muskets and rifles for another volley. Roger Lamb, a British soldier participating in the attack against the American right wing, recalled:

> When [we] arrived within forty yards of the enemy's line, it was perceived that their whole force had their arms presented, and resting on a rail fence . . . They were taking aim with the nicest precision. . . . At this awful period a general pause took place; both parties surveyed each other for the moment with the most anxious suspense. . . . Colonel Webster rode forward in the front of the 23d regiment, and said . . . "Come on, my brave Fuzileers!" This operated like an inspiring voice, they rushed forward amidst the enemy's fire; dreadful was the havoc on both sides.[44]

The American volley found its mark, and scores of Cornwallis's men fell. Captain Dugald Stuart of the 71st Highland Regiment noted that "one half of the Highlanders dropt on the spot."[45] Sir Thomas Saumarez of the Fusiliers remembered it as a "most galling and de-

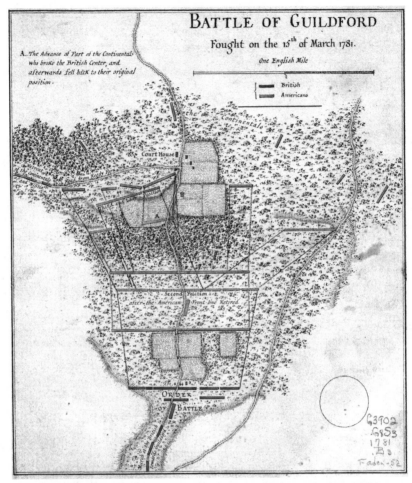

"Battle of Guildford [Guilford] fought on the 15th of March 1781." This map based on an earlier sketch and published in London in March 1787, shows the British forces led by Lt. Gen. Charles Cornwallis at the bottom and the three unlabeled defensive lines of Continental and militia troops above led by Maj. Gen. Nathanael Greene. The course of the battle is shown by the second and third positions taken by Cornwallis's forces. To the left of the Court House at the top, the counterattack led by Lt. Col. William Washington's light dragoons and the 1st Maryland Regiment is marked by the letter "A." Despite emerging victorious, the British suffered heavy casualties during the ninety minute battle. (*Library of Congress*)

structive fire."[46] The volley, though deadly, did not stop the British advance. Banastre Tarleton recalled that "the King's troops threw in their fire, and charged rapidly with their bayonets."[47] The remaining Americans in the first line were forced back as the British swept over the rail fence and continued toward Greene's next line, three hundred yards away.

General Greene's plan called for Lieutenant Colonel Washington and Lieutenant Colonel Lee to withdraw to the flanks of the third line, but Lee was forced to veer to the southeast, away from the American position. He soon found himself engaged in a completely separate struggle. His legion and Colonel Campbell's Virginia riflemen, along with 120 North Carolina militia who were swept along with Lee, faced a battalion of British Guards in a pitched battle in the woods. The fight quickly became confused as the heavily wooded terrain broke up units. Pockets of men fought from tree to tree in all directions. Cornwallis described this part of the battle.

> The excessive thickness of the woods rendered our bayonets of little use, and enabled the broken enemy to make frequent stands, with an irregular fire, which occasioned some loss . . . particularly on our right, where the 1st battalion [of Guards] and regiment of Bose [Germans] were warmly engaged in front, flank, and rear . . . with part of their extremity of their left wing.[48]

While a separate engagement raged on the far left on the second American line, over a thousand Virginia militiamen to Lee's right were engaged in their own desperate struggle to stop the British advance. The main British line approached Greene's second position with some difficulty; the dense woods broke up their formation.[49] As a result, British units attacked the Virginians in piecemeal fashion rather than in one continuous line. This reduced the shock value of Cornwallis's assault and helped the Virginians stand their ground. British historian Charles Stedman noted that "the second line of the enemy made a much braver and stouter resistance than the first. Posted in the woods, and covering themselves with trees, they kept up for a considerable time a galling fire, which did great execution."[50]

Lee recounted in his memoirs that the Virginians fought so well that they forced Cornwallis to commit all of his reserves: "Noble was the stand of the Virginia militia; Stevens and Lawson, with their faithful brigades . . . [caused] every corps of the British army, except the cavalry, [to be] brought into battle, and many of them suffered severely."[51]

Major St. George Tucker, an officer in General Lawson's militia brigade, was less complimentary of his men's effort. When word spread that the enemy had gained their right flank, most of Tucker's men fled to the rear. He rallied about seventy of them and engaged in an "irregular kind of skirmishing with the British, and were once successful enough to drive a party for a very small distance."[52] Tucker added that the men who stayed with him fired up to twenty rounds in the conflict, a significant number compared to the performance of the North Carolinians in the first line. Nonetheless, because most of his unit fled early in the engagement, Tucker was disillusioned by their conduct.

Greene, on the other hand, was pleased with the Virginia militia's conduct and noted the intensity of their effort in a letter to Congress. He declared, "The Virginia Militia gave the Enemy a warm reception and kept up a heavy fire for a long time."[53] He similarly informed Governor Jefferson that the British "were very much galled by an incessant fire [from the Virginia militia]."[54]

Most observers agreed that the Virginians fought well. Eventually, however, with General Stevens wounded in the thigh and British troops pressing their front and flanks, the Virginians were forced to retreat. They scurried back toward the last American line, pressed closely by the enemy.

Just as the British did at the second line, Cornwallis's troops arrived at Greene's third line in sections. The first to arrive was Lieutenant Colonel James Webster and the left wing of the British line. Instead of waiting for the right wing of the army to catch up, Webster unwisely led his brigade forward against Greene's Continentals. The British charged into a cleared ravine and then up a hillside toward the Americans. The Virginia and Maryland troops coolly held their fire until the British were at point-blank range and then blasted them with a murderous volley. Webster's brigade halted in its tracks, their commander seriously wounded in the leg, and retreated to the far wood line to await reinforcements.[55]

Additional British units arrived on Webster's right. British lieutenant colonel James Stuart led the Second Battalion of Guards against the left of the Continental line, which was held by the 2nd Maryland Regiment. The Marylanders fired a weak volley at the oncoming British and then inexplicably broke ranks and fled, leaving two cannon and the left flank of Greene's third line exposed. Greene reacted quickly to prevent a complete rout of his army, and ordered a retreat—but before the order was executed, Colonel John Gunby, commander of the 1st Maryland Regiment, "wheeled to his left upon Stuart, who was pursuing the flying second regiment."[56] One observer noted that "this conflict between the brigade of guards and the first regiment of Marylanders was most terrific, for they fired at the same instant, and they appeared so near that the blazes from the muzzles of the guns seemed to meet."[57]

Gunby's men followed their volley with a bayonet charge. At nearly the same moment, Colonel William Washington and his dragoons swept down on the British. The guards, who up to that point had kept their order, "were driven back with great slaughter" by the cavalry's sabers and the Marylanders' bayonets.[58] One Virginian horseman in particular, Peter Francisco, a giant of a man at six and a half feet tall, reportedly struck down numerous guardsmen before he was bayoneted in the leg.[59] The Maryland troops also inflicted great loss on the British. Lieutenant Colonel John Eager Howard, who took command of the First Maryland when Colonel Gunby was pinned under his horse, proudly recalled: "My men followed quickly, and we pressed through the guards, many of whom had been knocked down by the horse without being much hurt. We took some prisoners, and the whole were in our power."[60]

The bold charge of the First Maryland and Washington's cavalry briefly steadied the American left flank, but British artillery fire prevented the Americans from capitalizing on their success. As a result, Washington's cavalry and the Maryland Continentals disengaged and joined the rest of the American army in an orderly retreat from Guilford Courthouse. The British were too battered to vigorously pursue, so the battle came to a close.

Although Guilford Courthouse ended as yet another American defeat in the South, the victors had little to celebrate. Cornwallis lost over a quarter of his effective force, including many key officers. His army was exhausted and weak and in desperate need of rest and provisions. Three days after the bloody fight the British army limped south toward Cross Creek, where Cornwallis hoped to find much-needed provisions and loyalist support. He was disappointed on both counts, and bitterly complained to General Clinton in New York about the lack of Tory support: "Many of the inhabitants rode into camp, shook me by the hand, said they were glad to see us and to hear that we had beat Greene, and then rode home again . . . I could not get one hundred men . . . to stay with us even as militia."[61]

Cornwallis was equally disappointed at the lack of supplies that awaited him at Cross Creek: "I found to my great mortification and contrary to all former accounts that it was impossible to procure any considerable quantity of provisions and that there was not four days forage within twenty miles."[62]

The nearby Cape Fear River, which Cornwallis assumed could be used by the British navy to ferry supplies to Cross Creek, was unsuitable for such transport, so Cornwallis marched southward another eighty-five miles to Wilmington, which he reached on April 7. After ten weeks of near-continuous marching, Cornwallis and his men eagerly embraced the opportunity to rest and recover. It would be a brief respite, however, for to the south and north armed forces were on the move.

Events in southeastern Virginia were not nearly as bloody as they were in North Carolina, nonetheless General Benedict Arnold found himself (and his troops) in significant danger in March. General Muhlenberg's militia had become much more active, frequently probing Arnold's lines west of Portsmouth. Arnold's outpost at Great Bridge was also threatened by over a thousand Virginia and North Carolina militia under General Isaac Gregory of North Carolina.[63] This force was positioned to block Arnold's movement southward, something the notorious traitor might attempt once he learned that a French naval force with General Marquis de Lafayette and Continental reinforcements was due to arrive.

A curious incident occurred in the American camp at Great Bridge. A party of Colonel Josiah Parker's Virginia militia attacked and sank a British gunboat heading back to Portsmouth from Great Bridge. Among the items captured were the papers of Captain Stevenson of the Queen's Rangers, and among these papers were two letters curiously addressed to General Isaac Gregory, the American commander at Great Bridge. The letters suggested the existence of a plot by Gregory to surrender his troops to Arnold:

> G.G.
>
> Your well-formed plan of delivering those people now under your command into the hands of the British General at Portsmouth gives me much pleasure. Your next [letter] I hope will mention the place of ambuscade, and the manner you wish to fall into my hands.[64]

Colonel Parker was stunned. Writing to General Muhlenberg the same day the letters were discovered, Parker declared that the "contents embarrassed me amazingly [largely because] General Gregory had furnished the guards for the night.[65] [The General] was present when I examined the papers," continued Parker, "and declares himself innocent of any correspondence."[66] Although Gregory was regarded as a devoted patriot, so had Arnold been before his treason at West Point in the fall of 1780. With his trust in Gregory shaken, Colonel Parker quietly ordered his own guard detachments out to ensure the safety of the camp. General Gregory, eager to clear his name, welcomed his arrest two days later. In his absence, Colonel Parker assumed command of the rebel forces at Great Bridge.

Although Gregory remained under suspicion for weeks, it appears he was innocent of any plot to surrender his troops; according to Lieutenant Colonel Simcoe, Captain Stevenson's letters were fictitious, "written by way of amusement, and of passing the time."[67] Simcoe noted that his officers at Great Bridge were at first amused at the trouble the letters had caused Gregory, but when they learned that he had been placed under arrest, "Capt. Stevenson's humanity was alarmed," and he wrote to Colonel Parker to explain the origin of the letters and clear Gregory of any wrongdoing.[68] The damage to Gregory's reputation had already been done, however, and he did not return to command.

While Gregory's personal drama played out south of Portsmouth, Arnold—unconcerned about rumors of the French navy heading for Virginia to cut off his link with the sea—sent a large detachment of the 80th Regiment, as well as a few jaegers and cavalry, all under Lieutenant Colonel Dundas, across Hampton Roads on the evening of March 6, to surprise a body of militia that was reportedly in Hampton.

Conflicting accounts of what happened present a confused picture of the evening. According to Simcoe, who accompanied the detachment, the British initially failed to find any militia at Hampton, and settled for burning some supplies and large canoes. On their way back to their boats, however, the British encountered a party of two hundred militia, "drawn up on a plain, [with] a wet ditch in front."[69] Simcoe, who commanded the cavalry under Dundas, boldly charged the militia with only twenty-six horsemen. Simcoe speculated after the engagement that his small numbers actually emboldened the militia, who held their fire until the cavalry was within thirty yards, and then blasted Simcoe's horsemen with a volley. Simcoe recalled that "this checked us, and gave them time to [reload] and give us a second salute, but not with the same effect."[70] A number of riders where unhorsed, and some were hit by the gunfire, but enough remained mounted to break through the militia line and, reinforced by Dundas and the infantry (who followed on the heels of the cavalry at a jog), the British fell upon the militia with bayonets and swords, dispersing the rebels. Simcoe estimated that the enemy lost sixty men (killed,

Overleaf: "Part of the Province of Virginia." This undated map, c. 1791, is oriented with south at the top. It illustrates several key places in Gen. Benedict Arnold's invasion of Virginia, including New Port Nues (Newport News) where his invasion fleet first anchored, his outposts at Kemp's Landing and Great Bridge, his headquarters at Portsmouth, and Lynn Haven (Lynnhaven) Bay, where Gen. William Phillips anchored with reinforcements for Arnold's army. (*Library of Congress*)

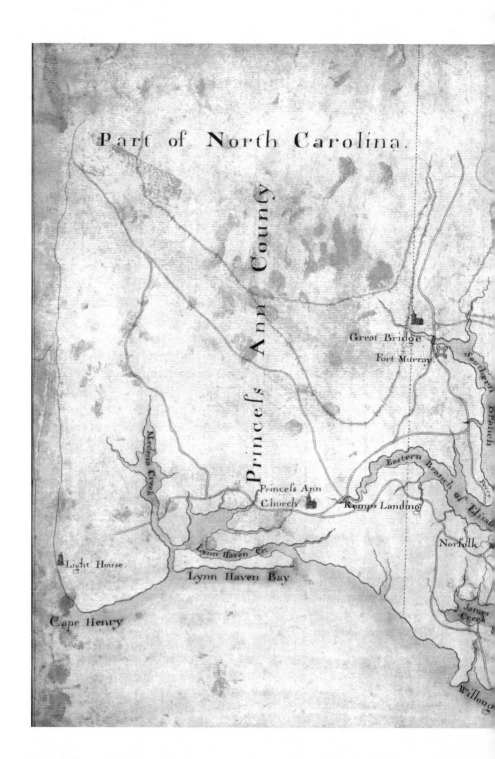

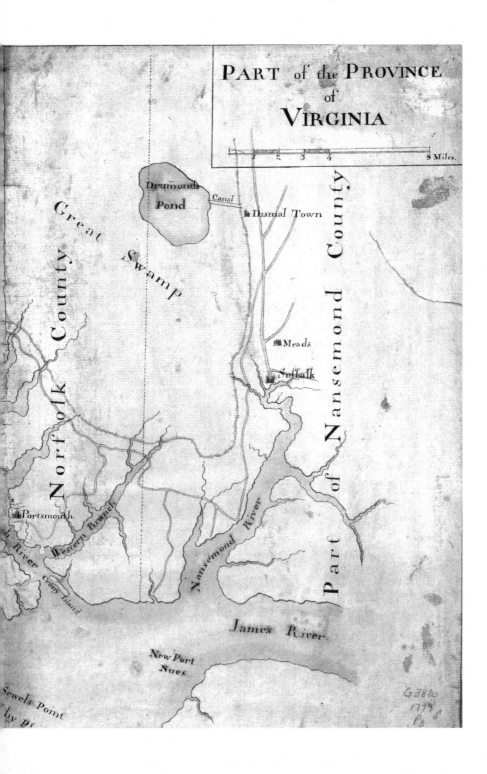

PART of the PROVINCE
of
VIRGINIA

8 Miles.

Drumonds
Pond

Canal

Dismal Town

Great Swamp

Norfolk County

Part of Nansemond County

Meads

Suffolk

Portsmouth

Western Branch

River

Cramp Island

Nansemond River

James River

New Port
Nues

Sewels Point
by De

wounded, and captured), compared to only a handful of losses for Dundas's troops.[71]

An account of the engagement in the *Virginia Gazette* claimed, however, that only forty militia confronted the British, and that they killed a British officer and two others and captured "five or six prisoners." The newspaper added that only a handful of the militia were lost.[72] Whatever the real numbers were, this engagement marked the end of Arnold's activity north of the James River.

With his troops back in Portsmouth, Arnold took measures to better secure his communication lines with his outposts at Great Bridge and Kemp's Landing. The notorious Major Weeks was active in the area again and threatened both outposts.[73]

In response to this development, Captain Ewald was ordered on March 10 to take his jaegers and a hundred additional soldiers, as well as all of the cavalry of the Queen's Rangers, and lie in ambush of Major Weeks. Around two o'clock the following morning gunfire erupted in the direction of Kemp's Landing, and Ewald led his detachment there. They had marched about two miles when his advance troops informed him that people were approaching his front. Ewald recalled that "hereupon I commanded, 'March! March! Lower bayonets!' whereupon a 'Who's there?' was heard, and the enemy fired a small volley. But at that instant, when I thought of fighting hand to hand with him, he scattered into the woods."[74]

From the prisoners Ewald captured he learned that he had just engaged the rear guard of Weeks. Apparently the Major was in the process of attacking the British outpost at Kemp's Landing when Ewald made contact with the rebel rear guard and forced Weeks to break off his attack.[75]

The threat to Great Bridge from the large rebel force posted south of the Elizabeth River proved insignificant to Arnold, and the next few days were rather quiet around Portsmouth and its outposts. The alarm was sounded again in Portsmouth on March 17, when a series of reports reached Arnold that warned of the impending arrival of a large French fleet. Ewald recalled that in Arnold's response to this news "General Arnold, who had constantly beaten the French and Americans at table, lost his head and wanted to make up all at once for what had been neglected up to now. We now worked hastily to make this post impregnable, although the entire place consisted of miserable works of only six to eight feet on the average."[76]

Ewald continued: "General Arnold, the former American Hannibal, now stayed on horseback day and night, galloped constantly from the fortified windmill up to the blockhouse on the left and back, and had a dam constructed across Mill Point Creek to create a flood in front of the right."[77]

The British warships that were still with Arnold—namely, the forty-four-gun *Charon*, twenty-eight-gun *Guadaloupe*, twenty-gun *Fowey*, several privateers, and a fire ship—were brought closer to Portsmouth, for both their own protection and that of the town. They anchored off of Mill Point and waited. Ewald, who was posted on the picket line at Scott's Creek guarding the road to Suffolk, remembered that "no one wanted to venture out of his hole to reconnoiter the enemy, and so we lived in anxiety for twenty-four hours."[78]

ARNOLD AND HIS MEN were right to be anxious, for the force that the Americans and French were sending to reinforce the Virginia militia (and ultimately to attack Portsmouth) was substantial. It included a powerful French fleet, to wrestle control of Hampton Roads from the British, and 1,200 of General Washington's best troops—light infantry from New England and New York—under the young French volunteer, the Marquis de Lafayette. The marquis had come to America in 1777 as a volunteer, enamored by America's cause, and, despite his youth, quickly won the confidence of Washington.

By 1781, General Lafayette commanded the American light infantry corps, and in February Washington ordered Lafayette and his corps southward to Virginia. They reached Annapolis, Maryland, on March 10, and halted, waiting for word that it was safe to proceed to Virginia by ship. The presence of British warships in the Chesapeake presented too great a danger to Lafayette's troops to sail down the bay in transports. Lafayette knew that a large French fleet was due to arrive in Virginia from Rhode Island to subdue Arnold's small naval force and clear the way for Lafayette's troops to proceed. While his troops waited in Annapolis for confirmation of the French navy's arrival, Lafayette sailed to Yorktown on a small, swift ship on March

14, and after a stop in Williamsburg crossed the James River and arrived at General Muhlenberg's camp at Sleepy Hole, on the Nansemond River, on March 19.

Lafayette was disappointed to learn that the French navy had yet to arrive and that the Virginian troops outside of Portsmouth were desperately short of ammunition. He reported that "no men had a Sufficiency [of ammunition] and Many Had None at All."[79] Unwilling to move all of Muhlenberg's poorly supplied force closer to Portsmouth, Lafayette settled for accompanying a detachment of riflemen and militia forward to reconnoiter Arnold's works.

MARCH 18 had been a tense night for Captain Ewald's jaegers on the picket line at Scott's Creek, just west of Portsmouth. The claim from a captured local inhabitant that five thousand men under Lafayette were marching toward Portsmouth rattled the nerves of Ewald's men.[80] As a precaution, the German jaeger commander sent a small party across the creek and down the road toward Suffolk to hide in ambush and give an early warning if indeed the captive's claims were true. Ewald apparently was not overly concerned, however, for he rode into Portsmouth the next morning to report to Arnold and accepted an invitation to dine with him. While he was changing his clothes in his quarters, Ewald heard gunfire in the direction of his picket troops at Scott's Creek. He recalled in his diary that "I had hardly dressed when I heard several rifle shots, and shortly afterward many shots in succession. I rushed toward my picket, and called to Lieutenant Bickell to send me a noncommissioned officer and sixteen jagers, in order to double the picket and to impede the enemy's passage over the causeway."[81]

When Ewald reached Scott's Creek he was shocked to find his picket troops gone and the entire opposite bank occupied by enemy riflemen, who commenced to fire upon him. Ewald recalled, "I found no picket, and was full of despair over the misbehavior of the noncommissioned officer of the picket. I dashed into the wood, where a short distance away I came across the [missing] jagers posted behind trees. With sword in hand I drove them toward the causeway again, where they fought like heroes in spite of the most frightful fire."[82]

Reinforced by another detachment of sixteen men, half of which deployed along the creek while the remainder defended the causeway with Ewald, they braced themselves for a rebel assault over the causeway. Ewald recalled that "during this time the [rebel] riflemen suddenly withdrew, and [the enemy] advanced in closed battalions against the causeway, but not a shot was fired. Despite all the efforts of their officers, however, they came no further than the entrance of the causeway, gave fire, and withdrew again. Fresh troops advanced each time, but they fared no better."[83]

Ewald's men kept up a hot and accurate fire, effectively blocking the causeway and bridge over Scott's Creek. In the midst of the fight, Ewald was struck by a musket ball just below the knee. He recounted, "I sat down and asked these eight brave men, of whom three already were wounded, not to leave their post, since the enemy could not come further as long as they stood firm."[84]

Lieutenant Alexander Bickell relieved Ewald, who was sent to the rear on a horse, where he met fifty men heading toward the creek to reinforce the picket. When he neared the earthworks of Portsmouth he met Arnold, who expressed his sorrow for Ewald's injury and asked whether the enemy would take the post at Scott's Creek. Ewald angrily remembered, "The question annoyed me, for he could see it all for himself. I said, 'No! As long as one jager lives, no damned American will come across the causeway!'"[85]

Ewald's pledge proved true; the Virginians never crossed the causeway, and disengaged soon after Ewald was wounded.

The engagement, which Lafayette described as trifling in his report to Washington, was certainly more significant to Ewald, and cost each side a handful of men. Ewald's picket detachment, including the ambush party that had been overrun by Lafayette's advance, was mauled, but the survivors and their commander took pride in holding back the rebels. Ewald recorded in his diary that "I rejoiced over the magnificent behavior of my brave jagers, who with all éclat had thus distinguished themselves before the eyes of the English. For surely one jager had fought against thirty Americans today."[86]

THE DAY AFTER the skirmish at Scott's Creek, General George Weedon, who had marched to Williamsburg a week earlier with militia troops from northern Virginia, wrote to Governor Jefferson with news that an unidentified naval squadron had arrived in Chesapeake Bay.[87] Weedon speculated that the ships were part of the long-expected French fleet, but the following day Commodore James Barron, in Hampton, informed the governor that the fleet was British.[88] British vice admiral Marriott Arbuthnot, with twelve powerful warships including the ninety-eight-gun HMS *London*, had prevailed in an engagement off the Virginia capes on March 16 against an equally powerful French naval squadron under the command of the Chevalier Destouches.

For nearly two hours the two fleets blasted each other with broadsides, inflicting extensive damage and a number of injuries, but sinking no ships. It was actually the British who broke off the engagement, but in doing so, they sailed into Chesapeake Bay while the French fleet headed back to their base of operations in Newport, Rhode Island, to refit.

The news grew worse for the Virginians on March 26, when the British naval presence in Lynnhaven Bay more than doubled with the arrival of a fleet of transport ships. Captain Richard Barron counted over thirty new vessels, and upon word of this General Steuben concluded what Virginia's authorities feared: that the transports were loaded with British reinforcements for Portsmouth.[89] These new troops, over two thousand strong, were commanded by General William Phillips, an experienced British commander who had been captured at Saratoga in 1777. His captivity included a brief stay in Virginia, until he was exchanged in the winter of 1781. The arrival of General Phillips and his men altered Lafayette's plans. The young Frenchman explained to Washington that

> the Return of the British fleet with vessels that Must Be transports from New York is a Circumstance which destroys Every Prospect of an operation Against Arnold. The Number of men is Not what I am afraid of [as] the French and Continental troops joined with the Militia must be Equal to a pretty Serious Siege, But Since the British fleet Have Returned and think

themselves Safe in this Bay, I entertain very little Hopes of Seeing the French flag in Hampton Road.[90]

With his hopes for a coordinated allied attack upon Arnold dashed, Lafayette headed back to Annapolis and proceeded to march north with his troops to rejoin Washington in New York. It would prove to be a premature move on his part.

Five

British Offensive Operations Resume in Virginia

APRIL–MAY 1781

O N APRIL 10, GENERAL CORNWALLIS, WHO HAD ARRIVED IN Wilmington, North Carolina, with his exhausted army just three days earlier, wrote to General Henry Clinton in New York to update Clinton on the situation (as Cornwallis knew it) in the South. In the letter, Cornwallis, who was unaware of the arrival of General Phillips and his troops in Virginia, declared that Virginia was the key to subduing the South, and confessed to Clinton that "I cannot help expressing my wishes that the Chesapeake may become the seat of war even (if necessary) at the expense of abandoning New York. Until Virginia is in a manner subdued our hold of the Carolinas must be difficult if not precarious."[1]

A week later, Cornwallis, still unaware of British troop increases in Virginia, reiterated his thoughts on Virginia's importance to Lord George Germain in London:

If . . . it should appear to be the interest of Great Britain to maintain what she already possesses and to push the war in the southern provinces I take the liberty of giving it as my opinion that a serious attempt upon Virginia would be the most solid plan, because successful operations might not only be attended with important consequences there but would tend to the security of South Carolina and ultimately to the submission of North Carolina.[2]

Cornwallis concluded his letter to Germain with subtle criticism of what he called Clinton's diversionary expeditions to Virginia: "The great reinforcement sent by Virginia to General Greene whilst General Arnold was in the Chesapeake are convincing proofs that small expeditions do not frighten that powerful province."[3]

Cornwallis finally learned of the arrival of General Phillips and his troops in Virginia four days after he wrote to Germain. Phillips's arrival (which was Clinton's response to Arnold's precarious situation at Portsmouth) brought British troop strength in Virginia to over four thousand men, more than twice the number of Cornwallis's battered army in Wilmington. Although reports from South Carolina warned that British control of that province was threatened by General Greene's return to South Carolina (and Cornwallis's absence), Cornwallis chose not to return to South Carolina. Instead, the British commander shifted his focus to Virginia.

Cornwallis wrote to General Phillips on April 24, and explained that since his weakened army could provide little assistance to the British outposts in South Carolina, he had decided to march north, some 240 miles, to join Phillips in Virginia. In doing so, Cornwallis left British control of South Carolina in the hands of Francis Lord Rawdon and the British and Tory troops scattered throughout the province.[4]

General William Phillips was well regarded and much admired in the British army. Captured at Saratoga in 1777, Phillips eventually found himself on parole in Charlottesville, Virginia, where he spent many pleasant hours with Governor Thomas Jefferson. Formally exchanged in late 1780, Phillips was sent back to the British army in New York, but soon returned to Virginia with nearly 2,500 troops to assume command of British forces there.

General Clinton instructed Phillips to take whatever measures he could to assist Cornwallis (whom Clinton assumed was still in North

Carolina completing the subjugation of that province to British authority). Like he had done with General Arnold and General Leslie, Clinton suggested that rebel magazines and supply depots along the James River and at Petersburg be destroyed, provided that the British post at Portsmouth not be placed in jeopardy. Clinton added that General Phillips was free to "carry on such desultory expeditions for the purpose of destroying the enemy's public stores and magazines in any part of the Chesapeake as you shall judge proper."[5]

Within days of his arrival in Virginia, Phillips acted on Clinton's instructions and sent a squadron of armed vessels, mostly privateers such as the *Trimer* and *Surprise* (which reportedly mounted from eighteen to twenty-four guns each), up the Potomac River.[6] The privateers were joined by at least one British warship, the sixteen-gun sloop *Savage*. The squadron's main objective was to obstruct General Lafayette and his light infantry corps (which was reportedly marching south again) from sailing down the Chesapeake Bay or crossing the Potomac River.[7] Lafayette had marched north with his light infantry from Annapolis following the arrival of Phillips, and had reached the Susquehanna River when he was ordered by General Washington to turn around and return to Virginia. Lafayette was to assume command of all the American troops in the Old Dominion and defend Virginia from the ever-growing British presence. The British naval squadron that sailed up the Potomac hoped to prevent, or at least delay, Lafayette's return to Virginia.

The British squadron also intended to raid the shores of both Virginia and Maryland and force Virginia's leaders to direct more attention, and presumably militia, to the Potomac. To accomplish this, the squadron dispersed at the mouth of the Potomac River. A few ships remained in the lower section of the river near the Chesapeake, and raided Northumberland County in Virginia and Saint Mary's County in Maryland, while the remainder of the squadron sailed up the Potomac River toward Alexandria.

By April 1, the *Trimer*, *Surprise*, and another unidentified sloop (probably the *Savage*) were anchored off Cedar Point, Maryland, about forty miles up the Potomac from the Chesapeake.[8] Just beyond Cedar Point, the river curved sharply westward and the wind, which blew from the northwest, made it difficult for the ships to sail any farther upriver, so they dropped anchor and sent a lone vessel, a tender belonging to the *Trimer* with a crew of twenty-one, ahead by oar to reconnoiter upriver.

Early in the morning of April 2, the British tender, with the help of the tide, arrived off Alexandria and attempted to seize a merchant ship loaded with tobacco in the harbor. Peter Wagner of Fairfax County recounted what happened: "A small Vessel came up to Alexandria and attempted to cut out of the Harbour a Baltimore Vessel lying there loaded with Tobacco. They boarded the vessel and had confined the men but being discovered by another Vessel in the Harbour the Town was alarmed which prevented the Enemy from carrying off the Vessel they had boarded."[9]

The privateersmen scrambled to return to their tender and escape downriver. They were pursued by two armed schooners that overtook them near Boyd's Hole in King George County.[10] In desperation, the privateersmen steered for the south shore of the Potomac. Colonel Henry Lee Sr., the county lieutenant of Prince William County (and father of "Light Horse" Harry Lee) reported that "as soon as the Schooner found she Must be taken the Men took to their boats and landed on the Virginia Side of the River. Sixteen of them were taken by the Inhabitants, eight of whom were sent to Fredericksburg from whence I hear they are sent to Winchester. The others were sent up in the Vessels that Pursued them to Alexandria and are Confined in that Gaol."[11]

One of the prisoners informed Lee of their intentions, had they escaped Alexandria undetected with the captured tobacco ship: "If the Enemy had Succeeded at Alexandria they intended; one of the Prisoners say, to have burnt Genl. Washingtons Houses, Plundered Colo. Mason and myself and endeavoured to have made me a Prisoner."[12]

Had the tender managed to flee just a few more miles downriver, past Mathias Point and the large bend in the river, they might have reached the protection of the *Trimer* and *Surprise*. Unaware, or perhaps unable to assist the tender due to the strong westerly wind that prevented the fleet from sailing around Mathias Point, the privateers at Cedar Point spent much of April 2 seizing tobacco from the warehouses along the Maryland shore. At some point in the day, probably at ebb tide, the fleet weighed anchor and moved downriver, stopping at Cole's Point in Westmoreland County to raid the property of Robert Carter and "seize" thirty of his slaves.[13]

The bulk of the privateer fleet returned upriver to Cedar Point on April 5 and focused its attention on the Virginia shore. Gerrard Hooes operated a ferry crossing in King George County, opposite from Cedar Point, and it became the next target of the raiders. John Skinker, the county lieutenant of King George County, reported to Governor Jefferson that evening: "Three large Schooners and some smaller Vessels of the Enemy [anchored] opposite Hoes Ferry. . . . About 8 o'clock at night [a party] landed at Mr. Garrard Hoes, plundered his House and what they could not carry away they utterly distroyd. They also took off 4 of his Negroes and set fire to his House."[14]

The British fleet continued further upriver, plundering other Virginia homes. Robert Washington of Choptank Creek, a relative of General Washington, lost four slaves and nearly all of his furniture, which was pillaged and destroyed by a party of privateers.[15] Maryland was not spared the wrath of the privateers; raiding parties landed across the Potomac, where they plundered and torched buildings indiscriminately.[16]

Although Virginia officials in Richmond were largely unaware of the severity of the raids and slow to respond, county leaders along the Potomac acted to defend their counties and neighbors. John Skinker assembled 260 armed militia at Boyd's Hole to protect the nearby tobacco warehouses and repel any attempted landing of the privateer crews.[17] Skinker lamented the shortage of arms for his men, writing to Governor Jefferson that "I am really sorry to inform your Excellency that not one third of my Militia have Arms fit for service."[18]

For a few days it was uncertain whether the militia upriver from Mathias Point actually needed to be alarmed or assembled; a strong northwesterly wind continued to prevent the privateer fleet from sailing any farther up the Potomac. By April 9, the fleet had actually dropped down the river again to Westmoreland County, where they sent raiding parties ashore near Stratford Hall. The raiders were confronted by Colonel Richard Henry Lee and the Westmoreland County militia. Lee recalled that he was with the Militia on the Shore of Potomac where we had a very warm engagement with a party of the enemy, about 90 men, who landed from two Brigs, a Schooner, and a smaller Vessel under a very heavy cannonade from the Vessels of War—the affair ended by the enemy being forced to reimbark with some haste . . . Their Vessels are yet near the Shore, and by a deserter . . . I learn that their Vessels with a ship of 20 guns now lying off, are bound up the river, as high as Alexandria to interrupt the passage of Troops across Potomac.[19]

By the next day, April 10, the fleet had returned upriver to Hooes Ferry. Colonel Edmund Reed was posted there with a detachment of volunteer cavalry from Caroline County, and reported that "this morning [the enemy] appeared [off] Mr. Hooes where I was Posted with my Dragoons and some few Militia . . . I followed them along shore to [Boyd's Hole] . . . The whole of the fleet amounted to two twenty-four gun ships, two Eighteen [gun ships], and six transports and tenders. They seem to be crouded with men."[20]

A shift in the wind finally allowed the British squadron to sail upriver around Mathias Point, and it passed Boyd's Hole without incident. Colonel Skinker watched them pass, and reported to Governor Jefferson that the fleet consisted of "4 Ships none less than 20 Guns, [plus] two Brigs and two Tenders."[21]

The fleet sailed through the evening and reached Alexandria by the morning of April 11. Robert Mitchell of Georgetown, Maryland, was in Alexandria, and described the town's reaction to the fleet's arrival: "Yesterday on my Arrival at Alexandria I found the town in much confusion occasioned by a small Fleet that appeared off the Town— say, three Ships, two Brigs and two Schooners. Two of the Ships appear to be of 18 Guns each, the other I cou'd not make out what number of Guns she mounted, but believe her to be a Frigate."[22]

Mitchell added a troubling comment: "The Lieutenant of the County expecting a sufficient number of Militia from the Country . . . to defend the Town had the colours hoisted in the Fort, but finding the Militia did not come In so fast as he had reason to expect, by the persuasion of the Inhabitants the colours were taken down."[23]

Mitchell's observation suggests that the townsfolk had decided not to fight. With so few armed militia in town, and appeals for help to the authorities of Prince George County across the river in Maryland falling on deaf ears (they had their own property to defend), it is not surprising that the townsfolk contemplated submission.

As it turned out, Alexandria was spared the trauma of a raid because the privateers never attempted to come ashore. They spent most of April 11 trying to free two vessels (one of the large ships and one of the brigs) that were grounded in shallow water just below the town.[24]

By the next day, militia reinforcements from the surrounding countryside emboldened Alexandria's defenders and dissuaded the privateers from landing. The privateers lingered a few miles below Alexandria, directing their attention to the Maryland shore, where they skirmished with the local militia and burned the plantation of Colonel Lyles (after he rejected a demand for fresh provisions for the fleet).[25]

On April 13, an incident occurred at Mount Vernon that absolutely appalled General Washington in New York. For nearly six years, General Washington's cousin, Lund Washington, had served as the caretaker of Mount Vernon in General Washington's absence. The commander in chief expressed complete faith in Lund's stewardship of his property, but Washington's trust in Lund was shaken when the American commander learned that his caretaker had entered into negotiations with the commander of the *Savage* over the return of a large number of runaway slaves from Mount Vernon. General Lafayette, who like Washington was greatly troubled by Lund's actions, informed Washington in late April that "when the Enemy Came to your House Many Negroes deserted to them. This piece of News did not affect me much as I little Value [slavery]— But You Cannot Conceive How Unhappy I Have Been to Hear that Mr. Lund Washington Went on Board the Enemy's vessels and Consented to give them provisions."[26]

Lafayette speculated that, as General Washington's representative, Lund's actions would "certainly Have a Bad effect, and Contrasts with Spirited Answers from Some Neighbours that Had their Houses Burnt Accordingly."[27]

General Washington received Lafayette's letter on May 4, five days after a letter from Lund arrived explaining his actions. General Washington had already responded to his cousin with a stern reprimand:

> I am very sorry to hear of your loss; I am a little sorry to hear of my own; but which gives me most concern, is, that you should go on board the enemys Vessels, and furnish them with refreshments. It would have been a less painful circumstance to me, to have heard, that in consequence of your non-compliance with their request, they had burnt my House, and laid the Plantation in ruins. You ought to have considered yourself as my representative, and should have reflected on the bad example of communicating with the enemy, and making a voluntary offer of refreshments to them with a view to prevent a conflagration . . . But to go on board their Vessels; carry them refreshments; commune with a parcel of plundering Scoundrels, and request a favor by asking the surrender of my Negroes, was exceedingly ill-judged, and 'tis to be feared, will be unhappy in its consequences, as it will be a precedent for others . . . Unless a stop to [the British raids occurs], I have little doubt of its ending in the loss of all my Negroes, and in the destruction of my Houses; but I am prepared for the event.[28]

Although Lund Washington's letter to General Washington has not been found, an account from the Marquis de Chastellux (a Frenchman travelling in Virginia in the spring of 1781 who had occasion to discuss the incident with Lund) claimed that

> Mr. Lund Washington, a relation of the General's and who managed all his affairs during his [long] absence with the army, informed me that an English frigate [the 16 gun H.M.S. *Savage*] having come up the Potomac, a party was landed who set fire to and destroyed some gentlemen's houses on the Maryland side in sight of Mount Vernon, the General's house; after which the Captain [Thomas Graves] sent a boat on shore to the General's demanding a large supply of provisions, etc. with a menace of burning it likewise in case of a refusal.[29]

The Marquis failed to mention Washington's loss of seventeen slaves (who fled to the British upon their arrival). He instead noted Lund Washington's defiant reply to the British commander. Lund informed Captain Graves that "when [General Washington] engaged in the contest he had put all to stake, and was well aware of the exposed situation of his house and property, in consequence of which he had given [Lund] orders by no means to comply with any such demands, for that he would make no unworthy compromise with the enemy, and was ready to meet the fate of his neighbors."[30]

This reply angered Captain Graves, and he positioned the *Savage* closer to shore as if to bombard Mount Vernon. At the same time, the British commander invited Lund aboard his ship to discuss matters further. Lund accepted (in hopes of regaining General Washington's slaves), and brought with him "a small present of poultry, of which he begged the Captain's acceptance." Lund told the Marquis that "his presence [aboard the *Savage*] produced the best effect, he was hospitably received notwithstanding he repeated the same sentiments with the same firmness. The captain expressed his personal respect for the character of the General."[31]

Captain Graves shrewdly assured Lund that nothing but his misunderstanding of Lund's defiant reply could have compelled him to "entertain the idea of taking the smallest measure offensive to so illustrious a character as the General."[32] In other words, Graves gave Lund a chance to reconsider his initial refusal to comply with Captain Graves's demands. This time Lund acquiesced to the British commander. The Marquis recorded that "Mr. [Lund] Washington, after spending some time in perfect harmony on board, returned [to Mount Vernon] and instantly dispatched sheep, hogs, and an abundant supply of other articles as a present to the English frigate."[33]

The gesture failed to gain the return of Washington's slaves, but it did preserve General Washington's home and buildings from destruction.

Across the river in Maryland, Colonel Lyles was not so lucky. A party of privateer sailors returned to his burnt-out estate in Prince George County and added insult to injury by stealing some hogs. They paid a steep price for them, however, for a body of militia challenged them and captured eleven of the raiders.[34] This marked the last significant action of the privateers; their two-week expedition up the Potomac River concluded with their departure from the river the next day.

The expedition's primary objective, to delay General Lafayette's movement southward, proved unnecessary, as Lafayette and his light infantry corps were still a hundred miles to the north on the banks of the Susquehanna River. The fleet's secondary objective, to spread destruction along the river, was fully achieved. The squadron met little resistance and suffered few losses, but inflicted thousands of dollars' worth of property damage and freed scores of slaves. Its presence on the Potomac also alarmed Virginia's militia forces in northern Virginia and reaffirmed the vulnerability of the state to attack by water.

Two weeks had passed since the privateer fleet had entered the Potomac River, during which time British activity in the rest of Virginia had remained relatively quiet. This was about to change, however, for General Phillips was determined to lead a powerful British force up the James River to disrupt the flow of men and supplies from Virginia to General Greene in South Carolina.

ON APRIL 18, over two thousand British troops under General Phillips sailed out of Portsmouth and up the James River.[35] Their destination was Williamsburg, where Phillips hoped to surprise a body of militia (estimated at six to eight hundred strong) in Virginia's former capital.[36] General Arnold accompanied Phillips, and reported to General Clinton in New York that the British force consisted of two battalions of light infantry, parts of the 76th and 80th Regiments, all of the Queen's Rangers, and approximately one hundred German jaegers, as well as Arnold's small American Legion corps.[37]

The British fleet of transports and warships was outpaced northward by rebel express riders, who spread the alarm of the British movement up both sides of the James River. Lieutenant Colonel James Innes, who had assumed command of the militia in Williamsburg upon General Thomas Nelson's prolonged illness in March, learned of the enemy's approach on the afternoon of April 18, and rushed word to Richmond, where Governor Jefferson received it the following morning. Jefferson immediately ordered the counties surrounding Richmond and Petersburg to call out all of their militia. Those from Henrico, Goochland, and Hanover were instructed to march to Richmond. Those from Powhatan and Cumberland were to march to Manchester (directly across the James River from Richmond), and the militia of Prince George, Dinwiddie, Amelia, and Chesterfield were ordered to gather in Petersburg.[38]

Back in Williamsburg, Lieutenant Colonel Innes prepared for the enemy's arrival. Over the course of April 19, the British flotilla anchored off Burwell's Ferry (the most likely landing spot for the British if Williamsburg was indeed their destination). From his position aboard a transport ship a mile offshore, Lieutenant Colonel Simcoe noted that "the enemy had thrown up entrenchments to secure the landing, and these appeared to be fully manned."[39] Whether this meant the Virginians intended to resist a British landing was to be determined the next day.

Lieutenant Colonel Simcoe and his Queen's Rangers led the British assault on Burwell's Ferry in the early afternoon of April 20. Escorted to shore by a single gunboat with a six-pound cannon on its bow, longboats transported the rangers straight for the ferry landing. About halfway to shore all of the long boats swung hard right. Assisted by the wind and tide, the sailors and troops rowed furiously downriver toward a creek a mile below Burwell's Ferry. The gunboat remained off of the ferry landing, and raked the shore with cannon fire to dissuade the militia at Burwell's from leaving their entrenchments and redeploying downriver to oppose Simcoe's landing. As a result, Simcoe and his rangers landed without opposition or loss.[40]

With their entrenchments flanked and the main force of General Phillips still to come ashore, the militia at Burwell's Ferry abandoned their post and withdrew to Williamsburg, just four miles inland. Although Lieutenant Colonel Innes was undoubtedly disappointed at the lack of fight in his troops, he was much more disturbed to learn (inaccurately, as it turned out) that "several armed vessels and 16 flat bottom Boats [had] proceeded up to James Town where . . . they have since Landed."[41] In truth, the British force in question had sailed past Jamestown to the Chickahominy River, where a portion of the troops under Lieutenant Colonel Dundas disembarked while the light infantry battalions under Lieutenant Colonel Robert Abercrombie continued up the Chickahominy River by boat towards the state naval shipyard.

Regardless of the inaccurate report about Jamestown Island, Lieutenant Colonel Innes realized that he now had two strong enemy forces on either side of him and risked becoming trapped. He reported to Governor Jefferson that "as soon as I found the Designs of the Enemy to circumvent me, I moved the troops to this place [Allen's Ordinary—six miles northwest of Williamsburg] which is the nearest position to the Town that can be taken with safety while the Enemy are masters of the water."[42]

Innes added that "the Troops under my Command are extremely harassed having laid upon their arms for upwards of fifty hours during such time they have received no Sustinance."[43]

While General Phillips and General Arnold settled into Williamsburg unopposed on April 20, Lieutenant Colonel Simcoe led forty cavalrymen on a dash to Yorktown to surprise a small garrison of rebel artillerists posted along the York River. Despite the need to take shelter from a fierce storm during the night (which prevented Simcoe from reaching Yorktown until morning), the small British party of horse surprised and routed the rebel garrison, some of whom escaped by boat across the York River. Simcoe spiked the abandoned cannon and rode back to Williamsburg to rejoin Phillips.[44] A few miles west of Williamsburg, Lieutenant Colonel Robert Abercrombie, against no opposition, destroyed the Virginia State Navy shipyard, along with the naval stores and vessels under construction on the Chickahominy River.

Disappointed that the militia had escaped up the peninsula, Phillips marched out of Williamsburg the next day (April 22) and reassembled his entire force at the mouth of the Chickahominy. They reboarded their transports and resumed their voyage up the James on April 23, passing Hood's Point (unmanned by the rebels) without incident. By April 23, they reached Westover, where they anchored.

Anxiety reigned in Richmond as Virginia's leaders scrambled to organize another defense of the capital. Only a small number of the summoned militia had arrived in Richmond; General Lafayette, with approximately nine hundred Continentals fit for duty, had only reached Alexandria (a hundred miles away), and Lieutenant Colonel Innes, with approximately seven hundred militia, had withdrawn across the Pamunkey River, some twenty-five miles northwest of Richmond. Innes explained his withdrawal to Governor Jefferson:

> Encumbered [with] upwards of one hundred sick and wounded, without Hospital Stores or Surgeons, burthened too with twenty waggons loaded with public Stores [and with troops] almost worn down with Fatigue and Hunger . . . [I crossed the Pamunkey and] shall now have it in my Power to dispose of the Invalids, give the Troops a little Refreshment, send the Baggage and Stores off to a Place of safety, and . . . march up towards Richmond with the Troops light, disencumber'd and refreshed.[45]

Upon news of the British fleet's initial movement up the James, General Peter Muhlenberg, who was encamped near Suffolk, had led approximately seven hundred militia northward. They marched thirteen miles on April 19 from their camp at Broadwater to Wall's Bridge, which spanned the Blackwater River. Darkness forced a halt, but upon word that the enemy fleet had anchored near Williamsburg Muhlenberg resumed his march the next day. He halted at Cabin Point on April 20, well above the British, and waited for General Phillips's next move. It came three days later, when the British fleet sailed past Hood's Point on its way to Westover.

The Virginians now realized that Phillips was heading for either Richmond or Petersburg. General Steuben had already ordered the military supplies and provisions amassed at Petersburg, Richmond, and Chesterfield Courthouse moved westward, and Governor Jefferson had ordered local militia to assemble at each location. When the British fleet anchored off of City Point at the mouth of the Appomattox River on April 24 and unloaded over two thousand troops and four cannon, it was finally clear where they were headed; their destination was Petersburg.

The town of Petersburg lay about twelve miles up the Appomattox River from City Point and served as an important supply depot for the Virginians. General Steuben defended Petersburg with approximately one thousand militia (Muhlenberg's seven hundred troops plus a few hundred local militia from Prince George, Dinwiddie, and Amelia Counties). Steuben explained his decision to oppose the vastly superior enemy at Petersburg to General Greene immediately after the battle:

> I had not more than One thousand men left to oppose the Enemies advance. In this Critical situation there were many reasons against risking a Total Defeat. The Loss of Arms was a principal one, & on the other hand to retire without some shew of Resistance would have intimidated the Inhabitants and have encouraged the Enemy to further incursions. This last consideration determined me to defend the place as far as our inferiority of numbers would permit.[46]

Outnumbered more than two to one, Steuben divided the militia into three detachments. A small detachment was posted to guard the bridge—and escape route—across the Appomattox River should the Virginians fail to stop the enemy advance (as expected). Two brass six-pound cannon covered the bridge from the heights above the north bank of the river, and a detachment of infantry supported the cannon at the bridge.[47]

About half a mile to the east of the bridge on the outskirts of Petersburg were two militia battalions (about five hundred men total) under Lieutenant Colonel Ralph Faulkner and Lieutenant Colonel John Slaughter. They were deployed behind a shallow, marshy creek (Lieutenant Run), their left flank anchored on the tobacco warehouses along the Appomattox River and their right anchored about five hundred yards to the south on rising ground upon the estate of Mrs. Mary Bolling.[48] A half mile to their front, on the eastern edge of the village of Blandford, were two additional militia battalions under Lieutenant Colonel Thomas Merriweather and Lieutenant Colonel John Dick. Approximately three hundred men strong, they were positioned on a small rise behind Poor's Creek and represented the first line of defense for the Virginians.[49] Small parties of militia were posted in advance of the first line to warn of the enemy's approach.

General Phillips and his force of over two thousand British troops (with four six-pound cannon) began their march from City Point to Petersburg around mid-morning on April 25. Eleven flat-bottomed boats armed with swivel guns and loaded with men and supplies advanced up the Appomattox River alongside the British column. Small militia parties posted in the neck of land between the James and Appomattox Rivers first noticed the enemy boats, and fired ineffectively at them.[50] The British continued on, and halted within a mile of Blandford around 2 P.M. to rest and refresh themselves.

Phillips could see the militia's first line deployed beyond Poor's Creek, and he realized his force significantly outnumbered the Virginians, so he formed his troops into a line of battle that extended well past the militia's right flank and ordered a frontal assault. Lieutenant Colonel Abercrombie led a battalion of light infantry and jaegers straight at the left wing of the militia line while Lieutenant Colonel Dundas struck their right with the 76th and 80th Regiments and tried to turn the rebel flank, forcing them to the river.[51]

Although they were indeed greatly outnumbered, the first militia line temporarily foiled Phillips's plan and gave up ground grudgingly. The Virginians used hedges, fences, and buildings for cover and kept up a hot fire on the British.[52] When the British boats in the river threatened to flank the left end of the first militia line, Colonel Faulkner at the second line rushed a company of militia to the river to confront the boats. Daniel Trabue, a Virginian soldier, recalled the incident:

> Colonel [Faulkner] called out for volunteers to go with him to take a britesh vesil that was 1/2 mile below and aground. . . . The company was made up and started in 5 Menuts. We went in a run, and before we got to them they fired on us. We went on the bank oppersit the vessil within 60 or 70 yards and fired on them as fast as we could load and shoot. They fired several times at us. When Capt. Epperson saw them putting their Mach to their cannon he would cry out, "Shot!" All of us would fall Down and the cannon ball generally went over our heads. We would Jump up and fire again at the men we could see on Deck and Did actually kill the most of them. . . . [Suddenly] Col.

[Faulker] came riding as fast as he could, hollowing, "Retreat! Retreat! Retreat!" We started and when he Met us he told us their was several hundred of the enemy a surrounding us. We run a long [way] up the river . . . to our redgement.[53]

The force of the British assault overwhelmed the first line of Virginians, nearly encircling them on their right flank, and they withdrew toward Petersburg before the British were able to cut them off completely.

The second militia line, partially reinforced by some of the more resolute troops from the first line, made an equally determined stand at Lieutenant Run on the edge of Petersburg. Private George Connolly claimed that he fired twenty-three rounds (possibly all the ammunition he carried in his cartridge box) before wounds forced him to retire.[54] Two British charges were repelled by the resolute Virginians, and General Phillips reportedly had to rely on his cannon to finally dislodge them. They withdrew northwestward toward the lone bridge across the Appomattox River.

With victory nearly complete, the British pressed the militia, but Steuben's rear guard used the town's warehouses and buildings for cover and maintained a hot fire that slowed their pursuit.[55] As the militia crossed the river, they fanned out on the other side to provide support for the beleaguered rear guard. Daniel Trabue remembered:

> As soon as we Got over the bridge we went above and below the bridge on the edge of the water to save the Retreat over the bridge. . . . When the enemy Discovered our men crossing the bridge they rushed after them. . . . The bridge was not wide

Overleaf: "Sketch of the Skirmish at Petersburg between the Royal Army under the command of Major Genl. Phillips, and the American Army commanded by Major Genl. Stewben [Steuben] in which the latter were defeated April 25th 1781," published by William Faden in 1784. The map shows the American forces positioned to the right of Blandford, who—in response to the Queen's Rangers's (no. 4 to the upper left) flanking movement (to no. 9, below Blanford, and then to no. 10 to the bottom right), retreated through the town and across the Apamatox [Appomattox] River (no. 8). (*Library of Congress*)

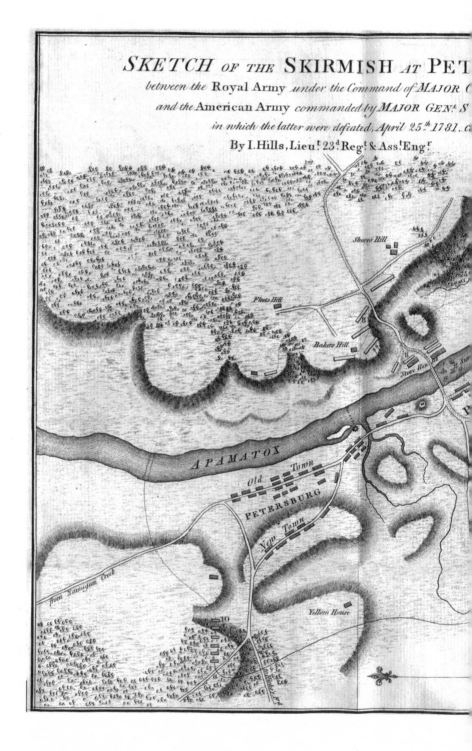

SKETCH OF THE SKIRMISH AT PET

beteween the Royal Army *under the Command of* MAJOR G.

and the American Army *commanded by* MAJOR GEN.l S.

in which the latter were defeated, April 25.th 1781. c

By I. Hills, Lieu.t 23.d Reg.t & Ass.t Eng.r

Shaees Hill

Fleets Hill

Bakers Hill

Store Hou.

APAMATOX

Old Town

PETERSBURG

New Town

from Namagean Creek

Yellow House

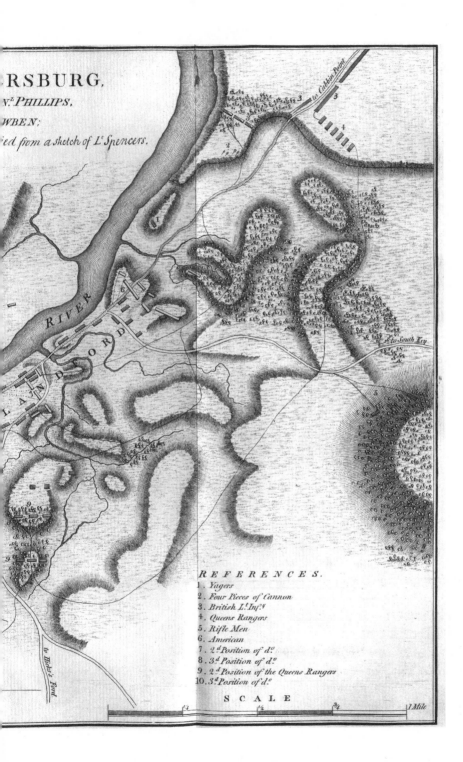

RSBURG,

N.º PHILLIPS,

WBEN:

ed from a sketch of L.ᵗ Spencers.

to Cabbin Point

to South Key

to Hicks's Ford

REFERENCES.

1. *Yagers*
2. *Four Pieces of Cannon*
3. *British L.ᵗ Inf.ʸ*
4. *Queens Rangers*
5. *Rifle Men*
6. *American*
7. *2.ᵈ Position of d.º*
8. *3.ᵈ Position of d.º*
9. *2.ᵈ Position of the Queens Rangers*
10. *3.ᵈ Position of d.º*

SCALE

¼   ½   ¾   1 Mile

enough for the men to get over fast enough. The enemy came Rushing Down to cut off our rear . . . charging with their bayonets. And our men resisted and Defended themselves some little, but at last they [captured] about 40 or 50 of our men before our faces within 60 or 70 yards of us but they paid dear for these men. Our regiment at the bridge fired 10 or 12 times each. I fired 13 very fair shoots. . . . And when I fired I looked where I shot at and I could see them tilt over. And when they [the British] Retreated up the hill from the bridge they run, as our men would keep on fireing at their flanks so as not to hurt our men who was Just made prisoners.[56]

The Virginians' heavy fire from the opposite riverbank, along with the removal of the bridge planks by the retreating militia, prevented the British from charging across the bridge.[57] Phillips's troops contented themselves with several parting cannon shots at the Virginians.

The Battle of Petersburg ended as expected: in a British victory. General Lafayette, who arrived in Richmond with Continental reinforcements and assumed command of all American forces in Virginia near the end of April, informed General Greene in South Carolina that "our loss it is said is about 20 killed and wounded."[58] General Muhlenberg, a participant in the fight, included troops captured by the enemy in his estimate of militia losses and declared that the total American casualties "will not exceed sixty."[59] Governor Jefferson reported a similar number to General Washington, noting that "our Loss was between sixty and seventy killed, wounded and taken." Jefferson added that the enemy's losses were probably equivalent, "as they broke twice and run like Sheep till supported by fresh Troops."[60]

Not surprisingly, British estimates of American casualties were much higher, with General Arnold and Lieutenant Colonel Simcoe both claiming a hundred militia killed and wounded. Arnold, writing to General Clinton on behalf of a gravely ill General Phillips in early May, reported British losses at Petersburg as only one man killed and ten wounded.[61] It's hard to believe, given the stubborn resistance of the militia at Petersburg, that the British suffered so few casualties, but all the British accounts of their losses at Petersburg describe them as trifling.

Although victory belonged to the British, Steuben and Muhlenberg were pleased that their outnumbered troops fought as well as they did.[62] Muhlenberg, who appears to have spent most of the battle within the militia lines east of the bridge, bragged to his brother that "every inch of ground to the bridge was warmly disputed. . . . The militia behaved with a spirit and resolution which would have done honour to veterans."[63] Steuben was equally complimentary of Muhlenberg, reporting to General Greene that "General Muhlenberg merits my particular acknowledgements for the good disposition he made & the great Gallantry with which he executed it."[64]

As night fell on Petersburg, Steuben led the militia northward toward Chesterfield Courthouse, ten miles above Petersburg. Phillips did not pursue, and spent the night at Petersburg, satisfied that his army had driven the Virginians from an important rebel supply depot. The British lingered in Petersburg another day, burning some tobacco warehouses along the river (along with four thousand hogsheads of tobacco) and a few small boats, but sparing the town from destruction.[65]

On April 27, Phillips marched his army across the Appomattox, dividing his force. Arnold led the 76th and 80th Regiments, the Queen's Rangers, his own American Legion, and part of the jaegers toward Osborne's Landing, ten miles north of Petersburg on the James River, to challenge the remnants of the Virginia State Navy. Phillips led the remainder of his force, which included two battalions of light infantry, the cavalry of the Queen's Rangers, and the rest of the jaegers, to Chesterfield Courthouse, the muster point for Virginia's Continental recruits.[66] Over 150 log huts capable of housing two thousand recruits had been constructed there, but when Phillips arrived he found the encampment deserted. Steuben had moved on to Richmond to rendezvous with Lafayette and his Continental reinforcements. Phillips contented himself with burning the huts and destroying three hundred barrels of flour.[67]

WHILE PHILLIPS raided Chesterfield Courthouse, Benedict Arnold approached Osborne's Landing to confront the bulk of Virginia's state navy. The potential firepower of the small flotilla at Osborne's Landing was impressive, and included the eighteen-gun *Apollo*; two sixteen-gun ships, the *Tempest* and *Renown*; the fourteen-gun *Jefferson*; and several other vessels.[68] Fully manned, these ships held nearly seven hundred men, but desertions and the lack of new recruits meant that only seventy-eight men were on duty.[69] Just five men crewed the *Apollo*, and only six were aboard the *Tempest*. Both ships, when fully manned, held crews of 120 each.[70]

This undermanned force, along with a few hundred Virginia militia on the northern bank of the James, confronted Arnold's force around noon on April 27. Arnold hoped the rebel commander would realize the futility of resistance, and sent a flag of truce to Captain William Lewis demanding the flotilla's surrender. Lewis spurned the demand and vowed to fight.[71] Arnold brought two three-pound and two six-pound cannon to a bluff overlooking the ships and commenced a bombardment of them. At the same time, a detachment of jaegers positioned themselves on a bluff overlooking the anchorage to sweep the rebel decks with their rifles. The rest of Arnold's force pitched in with musket fire.[72]

The Virginians fought back, but their fire was ineffective. The cannon onboard the ships could not elevate their fire high enough to reach the bluff, and the Virginia militia on the opposite shore were too far away to fire effectively at Arnold's men. When a lucky British artillery shot cut an anchor cable on the *Tempest* (causing the ship to drift and expose the crew to fire from bow to stern), her skeleton crew abandoned her. This sparked panic among the other ships. Some crews scuttled their vessels; others torched their ships, while the remainder simply abandoned them to Arnold. As the state navy sailors scrambled to reach the northern bank of the river, some of Arnold's men moved to seize the abandoned and damaged ships as prizes. Lieutenant Colonel Simcoe proudly described how one of his officers captured two ships:

> The enemy had scuttled several of their ships, which were now sinking; others, boarded by the intrepid Lt. Fitzpatrick, were on fire; and although cannon and musketry from the opposite shore, kept up a smart fire on him, that active officer rowed on. He put three men on board one ship, and cut her cable, and he left . . . three more in another and attained himself

the headmost, whose guns he immediately turned upon the enemy.[73]

Although the loss of the state naval fleet was complete, most of the sailors, along with the militia posted on the north bank of the river, escaped. The bulk of Virginia's state navy was destroyed in less than an hour without the loss of a single British soldier.[74]

General Phillips joined Arnold at Osborne's Landing (seven miles east of Chesterfield Courthouse) a few hours after the engagement, and the British troops spent the next two days repairing some of the captured vessels. On April 30, Phillips marched north toward Richmond, halting in Manchester (a village directly across the James River from Richmond), where his troops destroyed 1,200 hogsheads of tobacco. General Lafayette, who had reached Richmond the day before with nine hundred Continental soldiers, observed the destruction from across the river.[75] With Steuben and most of the militia a day's march northwest of the capital, and Lafayette's cannon and baggage yet to arrive in Richmond, there was little Lafayette could do except post troops on the heights of Richmond, summon Steuben to join him with the militia, and hurry along his artillery and baggage train.

Upon observing Lafayette's troops deployed on the heights overlooking the capital and river, Phillips, unaware of Lafayette's lack of cannon, canceled his planned attack on Richmond. Lafayette bemusedly reported to General Washington that an observer with Phillips claimed the British general "flew into a Violent passion and Swore Vengeance against [Lafayette]," as he ordered his army to march southward from Manchester to rejoin the British transport ships at City Point.[76]

Phillips and his army boarded the transport ships on May 2 and proceeded downriver. They sailed as far as Hog Island when, on May 7, Phillips received General Cornwallis's April 24 letter instructing Phillips to rendezvous with Cornwallis at Petersburg. Phillips immediately changed course and sailed back upriver to Brandon Plantation in Prince George County, where the bulk of his force disembarked and marched twenty-five miles to Petersburg. The British light infantry battalions and part of the Queen's Rangers continued upriver by ship to City Point and marched to Petersburg from there. By May 10, Phillips and his army were quartered in Petersburg, waiting for Cornwallis and his force of 1,500 men to arrive from North Carolina.

Benedict Arnold in a miniature portrait wearing a British army uniform. (*Private Collection*)

Thomas Jefferson in a miniature portrait by John Trumbull. (*Monticello*)

Detail from a British eighteenth-century engraving showing landing craft of the type used by Benedict Arnold's forces during their invasion of Virginia. (*Library of Congress*)

Charles Cornwallis in an engraving based on Daniel Gardner's c. 1780 portrait. (*New York Public Library*)

Nathanael Greene by Charles Willson Peale, 1783. (*National Park Service*)

Lynn Haven [Lynnhaven] Bay, near Norfolk, Virginia, where Gen. William Phillips anchored with reinforcements for Arnold's army, on March 26, 1781. (*New York Public Library*)

John Graves Simcoe in an engraving based on John Forster's portrait of Simcoe as Lieutenant Governor of Upper Canada. (*New York Public Library*)

Henry Lee by Charles Willson Peale, c. 1782. (*National Park Service*)

Banastre Tarleton by Sir Joshua Reynolds, 1782. (*National Portrait Gallery*)

Marquis de Lafayette by Francesco Giuseppe Casanova, c.1781-85. (*New-York Historical Society*)

Mount Vernon, Virginia, George Washington's estate by Frances Jukes, c. 1800. (*New York Public Library*)

"Peter Francisco's gallant action with nine of Tarleton's cavalry in sight of a troop of four hundred men," from a drawing by John Barralet, c. 1814. This illustration depicts Francisco during a period when he was convalescing after the Battle of Guilford Courthouse where he had been wounded (see page 80). (*Library of Congress*)

Johann Ewald in his Danish general's uniform following the American Revolution. (*Frederiksborg Castle, Denmark*)

Friedrich Wilhelm von Steuben by Charles Willson Peale, 1780. (*Pennsylvania Academy of the Fine Arts*)

Anthony Wayne in an engraving after a sketch by John Trumbull. (*New York Public Library*)

William Phillips in an engraving after a print by V. Green. (*New York Public Library*)

Daniel Morgan in an engraving after
John Trumbull.
(*New York Public Library*)

Peter Muhlenberg in an engraving after
John Trumbull.
(*New York Public Library*)

Henry Clinton in a miniature by John
Smart, 1777.
(*National Portrait Gallery*)

Otho Williams in an engraving after
Charles Willson Peale.
(*New York Public Library*)

Six

Cornwallis Comes
to Virginia

MAY–JUNE 1781

G ENERAL CHARLES CORNWALLIS FIRMLY BELIEVED THAT VIRGINIA,
which had long provided a large number of troops and supplies to General Greene's army in the Carolinas, was the key to victory in the South, and he was determined to unite his small force with
General Phillips in Petersburg, subdue the Old Dominion, and end
Virginia's support for Greene. Cornwallis embarked on the 240-mile
march to Petersburg in late April and met little resistance along the
way.[1] He had with him about 1,600 men from the 23rd and 33rd
Regiments, the Brigade of Guards, a battalion of the 71st Regiment,
the Hessian von Bose Regiment, Tarleton's Legion, several detached
light infantry companies, and four cannon.[2]

While Cornwallis and his army marched north from Wilmington,
General Lafayette spent the first half of May reacting to the movements of General Phillips. When Phillips sailed down the James River
in early May, Lafayette marched his force of Continentals (reduced
to eight hundred effectives due to illness) fifteen miles east of Rich-

mond to Bottoms Bridge in anticipation of a possible march to Fredericksburg to defend Hunter's Iron Works.[3] Lafayette speculated to General Washington that "having Missed Richmond Mr. Hunter's works at Fredericksburg Must Be their Next object as they are the only support of our operations in the Southward."[4]

Lafayette expected Phillips to sail his force into the Chesapeake Bay and then up the Potomac or Rappahannock River to strike Fredericksburg. Of course, Phillips might also move against Williamsburg again, or return to Portsmouth, so militia detachments were sent downriver to guard against those possibilities.[5] Until Lafayette was sure of Phillips's destination, he remained encamped at Bottom's Bridge, ready to march in multiple directions.

Reports that Phillips had actually reversed direction on the James River and returned to Petersburg prompted Lafayette to march his army to Osborne's Landing (via Richmond). Lafayette did so with a sense of foreboding, for recent letters from North Carolina informed him that Cornwallis was marching north to join Phillips. Lafayette discussed his concern in a letter to his friend, the Chevalier de La Luzerne:

> My situation . . . cannot help being a bit confining. When I look to the left, there is General Phillips with his army and absolute command of the James River. When I turn to the right, Lord Cornwallis's army is advancing as fast as it can go to devour me, and the worst of the affair is that on looking behind me I see just 900 Continental troops and some militia, sometimes more and sometimes less but never enough to not be completely thrashed by the smallest of the two armies that do me the honor of visiting.[6]

With Phillips (who was gravely ill) and his force securely in Petersburg awaiting the arrival of Cornwallis, Lafayette withdrew back across the James River on May 10 and encamped at Wilton Plantation, the estate of William Randolph, to await developments. On May 15, Lafayette bemoaned the situation confronting him to General George Weedon of Fredericksburg: "The Arrival of the Ennemy at Petersburg, their Command of the James and Appomattox River, the approach of Lord Cornwallis . . . Such are the Reasons which Render our Situation precarious and with the Handful of Men I have, there is No chance of Resisting the Combined Armies unless I Am Speedily and powerfully Reinforced."[7]

Just such a reinforcement of Pennsylvania Continentals under General Anthony Wayne had been ordered to Virginia weeks earlier, but morale and transport problems delayed their march, and it would be another month before they joined Lafayette. In the meantime, the young French commander of American forces in Virginia had to organize some sort of resistance to the soon-to-be-reinforced and vastly superior enemy in order to maintain patriot morale in the state. The trick was to do so without risking his small army, which Lafayette reported on May 18 amounted to approximately 900 Continentals, 1,200 militia, 6 artillery pieces, and a handful of cavalry.[8]

THE ARRIVAL OF Cornwallis and his 1,600 troops in Petersburg on May 20 swelled the number of British troops in central Virginia to nearly 5,000. Within days, additional reinforcements from New York arrived, bringing Cornwallis's total force in Virginia (including the garrison at Portsmouth) to over seven thousand troops.[9] Circumstances had developed nicely for Cornwallis, but there was one significant setback. A week before he reached Petersburg, Cornwallis's friend and subordinate, Phillips, succumbed to his illness and died. Benedict Arnold had assumed command upon the death of General Phillips, but soon after Cornwallis arrived Arnold returned to Portsmouth and then sailed to New York; according to Banastre Tarleton, "business of consequence demanded his attention."[10]

Across the James River at Wilton Plantation, Lafayette reacted to the arrival of Cornwallis by moving his army to Richmond. On May 22, he candidly described the challenge before him to the Chevalier de La Luzerne:

We are still alive, Monsieur le Chevalier, and so far our little corps has not received the terrible visit. . . . The proportion of [the enemy's] regular infantry to ours is between four and five to one and their cavalry ten to one; there are a few Tories, with whom I hardly bother. Our militia is not very numerous on paper, and it is even less so in the field. We lack arms, we haven't a hundred riflemen, and if we are beaten, that is to say if we are caught, we shall all be routed. The militia is used to advantage in the North, but in this country there are so many roads that one's flanks are constantly exposed wherever one turns. We must maneuver, we must reconnoiter, and all that (especially without cavalry) is very difficult for us.[11]

Four days later, Cornwallis, who had moved his army across the James River to Westover, revealed his plan for Virginia in a long-overdue letter to General Clinton in New York: "I shall now proceed to dislodge La Fayette from Richmond, and with my light troops destroy any magazines or stores in the neighbourhood which may have been collected either for his use or for General Greene's army."[12]

Dislodging Lafayette from Richmond proved a simple task. The American commander had no interest in an engagement with Cornwallis, so when the British army (approximately five thousand strong) broke camp from Westover on May 26 and marched northwestward to Turkey Island Creek (about twelve miles from Richmond), Lafayette and his outnumbered army abandoned the capital and marched north, away from Cornwallis.

When the British army changed direction and swung directly north toward Bottoms Bridge, Lafayette concluded that Hunter's Foundry in Fredericksburg was Cornwallis's target. He informed Governor Jefferson on May 28 that

the Enemy's intention has been to destroy this army and I conjecture would have been afterwards to destroy the stores which it covers. They have now undertaken another movement and it appears they are going through the country to Fredericksburg. Their Dragoons were this morning near Hanover Court House and (unless this is a feint) I expect the Army will be there this evening.[13]

Recognizing that he was powerless to stop Cornwallis, Lafayette added: "We shall be upon a parallel line with the Enemy keeping the upper part of the Country." But with "no Riflemen, no Cavalry, no arms, and few Militia coming," Lafayette conceded that there was little he could do to stop Cornwallis.[14]

Lafayette settled for hovering on Cornwallis's left flank to try to deter the British commander from striking west, while simultaneously closing the gap between his overmatched troops and the 1,200 Pennsylvania Continentals marching southward under General Anthony Wayne. Lafayette hoped that the addition of Wayne's troops would give his outnumbered American army a better chance, slim though it might be, of success against Cornwallis when the time came to fight. Until Wayne and his troops arrived, however, Lafayette was determined to avoid a general engagement with Cornwallis.

The challenge was to do this without appearing weak and ineffectual—hence Lafayette's measured movements on a parallel track with the British. When Cornwallis marched north, as he did on May 29 and 30 to Newcastle and Hanover Courthouse, Lafayette followed suit, marching to Scotchtown and Anderson Bridge on the North Anna River. Along the way Lafayette appealed to Generals Steuben, Weedon, and Wayne, as well as Governor Jefferson (whose term was about to end), of his movements, hoping for reinforcements. As he drew closer to Fredericksburg in late May, it appeared that Lafayette would finally get his wish and be joined by a large detachment of militia. On May 31, he reported to Jefferson that "tomorrow I form a junction with Gen. Weedon at Mattopony church and should General Waine Arrive our Inferiority will not Be quite So alarming. . . . Lord [Cornwallis] is going from His friends and we are going to Meet ours."[15]

Alas, Weedon and his reinforcements never arrived. General Weedon sheepishly wrote to Lafayette to explain their absence:

> I intended moving to-night with the small handful of men at this place, but not being able to remove the stores and disperse the tobacco . . . [from Fredericksburg, I] have risked your censure for the completion of this object, well knowing that a few men added to your operating force, could have but small weight in anything decisive.[16]

Lafayette marched a few miles farther northwest to Corbin's Bridge on June 2, and encamped southwest of Fredericksburg along the Po River.

Although Cornwallis ordered some of his cavalry and light troops across the North Anna River as far as Bowling Green in early June (just twenty-five miles south of Fredericksburg), the British commander's focus swung suddenly westward on June 2, away from Fredericksburg and Lafayette. Lieutenant Colonel Banastre Tarleton claimed years later in his recollections of the American campaign that, when Cornwallis learned that the Virginia General Assembly and Governor Jefferson had gathered in Charlottesville, and that Baron von Steuben with a detachment of Continental levies guarded important military stores at the Point of Fork on the James River, Cornwallis decided to end his march to Fredericksburg and instead send two strong detachments westward ahead of his army to strike Charlottesville and Point of Fork.[17] Cornwallis explained his rationale for ending his march to Fredericksburg to General Clinton:

> By pushing my light troops over the North Anna, I [threatened both] Fredericksburgh, and . . . [Lafayette's] junction with General Wayne, who was then marching through Maryland. From what I could learn of the present state of Hunter's iron manufactory, it did not appear of so much importance as the stores on the other side of the country, and it was impossible to prevent the junction between the Marquis and Wayne: I therefore took advantage of the Marquis's passing the Rappahannock, and detached Lieutenant-Colonel Simcoe and Tarleton to disturb the assembly then sitting in Charlottesville, and to destroy the stores there, at Old Albemarle court house, and the Point of Fork.[18]

Cornwallis sent Lieutenant Colonels Simcoe and Tarleton with their detachments westward, and trailed behind them with the rest of his army.

It took a couple of days for Lafayette to realize Cornwallis's sudden shift in strategy. He had continued to march north, across the Rapidan River into Culpeper County, hoping to unite with General

Wayne's reinforcements at any moment. The Pennsylvanians were still a week away, however, and when Lafayette finally realized that Cornwallis had diverted his army westward to threaten Virginia's political leaders and the important military stores stockpiled at Point of Fork, he adjusted his own march route southwestward, sending word to Wayne to catch up to him as quickly as possible.

Lafayette still recognized that his army was too weak to directly challenge Cornwallis, but he wanted to position it so that when he was finally reinforced by Wayne he might be able to defend some of the military stores in central Virginia. Unfortunately, it was too late to protect the state legislators in Charlottesville or the military stores at Point of Fork; Tarleton and Simcoe had already reached those places.

ON JUNE 3, Lieutenant Colonel Banastre Tarleton, with 180 legion dragoons and 70 mounted infantry of the 23rd Regiment, dashed westward across Hanover and Louisa Counties toward Charlottesville.[19] The rapid pace and heat of the day forced Tarleton to halt at midday to refresh his men and horses, but they soon returned to their saddles, where they remained for the rest of the afternoon and most of the evening. They rested again near Louisa Courthouse at 11 P.M. but were back on the road by 2 A.M., determined to surprise Governor Jefferson and the Virginia General Assembly.[20]

Fortunately for the Virginians, Tarleton's force was observed by twenty-six-year-old Jack Jouett a few miles east of Louisa Courthouse at the Cuckoo Tavern. Jouett quickly deduced Tarleton's destination and slipped away, riding approximately forty miles over back roads and country paths to warn Jefferson and the legislators of Tarleton's approach. Jouett rode first to Jefferson's home at Monticello, which sat upon an 850-foot-high mountain overlooking Charlottesville. Staying with Jefferson and his family were Archibald Cary and Benjamin Harrison, Speakers of the House of Delegates and State Senate, as well as Thomas Nelson Jr., Jefferson's soon-to-be-successor as governor.

The entire household was roused from their beds at dawn by Jouett, whose face was streaked with scratches and blood from the numerous branches and briars he encountered on his ride to Monticello.[21] Jefferson received Jouett's news calmly and insisted that there was time for breakfast.[22] While Jefferson and his family and guests took breakfast, Jouett rode to Charlottesville to warn the town and the rest of the Assembly.

Going door to door to spread the alarm, Jouett was initially met with skepticism and disbelief.[23] Most legislators assumed that Charlottesville was beyond Cornwallis's reach. Jouett's earnestness soon convinced them that they were in danger, and they reluctantly decided to adjourn and reconvene the Assembly in a week on the other side of the Blue Ridge Mountains in Staunton.[24] Most then hurriedly packed their belongings and fled westward over the mountains. House Speaker Harrison recalled that the bulk of the legislators "had not left town an hour before [Tarleton] entered," and credited Jouett (without naming him) for the Assembly's escape.[25] "Had it not been for the extraordinary exertions and kindness of a young gentleman who discovered [Tarleton's] intentions and got round [his force] in the night, not one man of those in town would have escaped; as it was, so incredulous were some of us, that it was with much difficulty [that the Assembly] could be prevailed on to adjourn."[26]

Not all of the legislators made it out of town before Tarleton arrived; a handful, including Daniel Boone, the noted frontiersman, tarried too long and were seized. Many more legislators would have been captured had Tarleton not stopped outside of Charlottesville to destroy a small wagon train of Continental supplies heading to the Carolinas. Another stop at Dr. Thomas Walker's plantation at Castle Hill (a few miles from Charlottesville) also cost Tarleton precious time. Tarleton seized some of Dr. Walker's guests, including a South Carolina delegate to the Continental Congress and two members of the Virginia House of Delegates, and continued on to Charlottesville.

Tarleton's advance guard of dragoons was met on the outskirts of Charlottesville by approximately a hundred local militia who guarded the ford across the Rivanna River. Tarleton recalled that he ordered an immediate attack, and "the cavalry charged through the water with very little loss and routed the detachment posted at that place."[27] The bulk of Tarleton's force rushed into town "to continue the confusion of the Americans, and to apprehend, if possible, the governor and assembly."[28]

Unsure of Jefferson's location, Tarleton sent a separate detachment to Monticello under Captain Kenneth MacLeod to search for the governor. Jefferson, who had lingered at his home after his guests and family had fled, observed Tarleton's arrival in Charlottesville through a spyglass and realized it was time to leave.

As MacLeod and his men made their way up the winding road to Monticello, Jefferson fled his estate in the opposite direction on horseback, "plunging into the woods of the adjoining mountain."[29] He escaped unnoticed by mere minutes. While MacLeod and his men searched the mansion and grounds, Jefferson continued through the woods until he came to the road that his wife and children had fled on and soon caught up with their carriage. They all continued on to John Coles's estate at Enniscorthy.[30] Fortunately for Jefferson, Captain MacLeod obeyed Tarleton's instructions to spare Monticello of any damage, and Jefferson's estate escaped unscathed from the British intruders.

Thwarted in his goal of capturing Jefferson as well as key members of Virginia's legislature, Tarleton had to settle for dispersing the Virginia Assembly (which disrupted Virginia's war efforts) and destroying "a great quantity of stores," including— claimed Tarleton— nearly four hundred barrels of powder and one thousand new muskets that had been abandoned by the routed Virginians.[31] Tarleton was also pleased to "liberate" twenty British soldiers from General Burgoyne's captured army at Saratoga.[32] They had somehow remained in the area after the bulk of the convention prisoners were sent to Winchester, and when they learned of Tarleton's presence in Charlottesville they reported to the British commander. Tarleton speculated that many more prisoners would have joined him if he had remained in Charlottesville beyond the one night he spent there.[33] Alas, his instructions were to join Lieutenant Colonel Simcoe at Point of Fork, so he departed on the afternoon of June 5 and headed east.

At almost the same moment that Tarleton left Charlottesville, Lieutenant Colonel John Simcoe was securing a large cache of military stores that his troops had seized from General Steuben at Point of Fork, twenty-five miles southeast of Charlottesville. This supply depot, located at the juncture of the Rivanna and Fluvanna Rivers (which came together to form the James River), was an important staging area for Virginia troops and supplies bound for General Greene's army in South Carolina.

Cornwallis wanted to disrupt the flow of reinforcements and supplies to Greene, so he sent Simcoe to raid Point of Fork on the same day that he ordered Tarleton to strike Charlottesville. Simcoe's force included his own Queen's Rangers (reduced to two hundred worn-down infantry and a hundred cavalry) along with a battalion of the 71st Regiment, detachments of jaeger and loyalist riflemen, and one three-pound cannon and crew.[34] Simcoe's force, which was mostly on foot, conducted several long marches of twenty-five to thirty miles a day through Hanover and Goochland Counties to reach Point of Fork by June 4. Simcoe recalled that "the incessant marches of the Rangers . . . had so worn out their shoes, that . . . it appeared that near fifty men were absolutely barefooted."[35]

Encamped at Point of Fork and unaware of Simcoe's approach were approximately 550 Continental levies (new recruits) and over 300 recently arrived militia.[36] Steuben had planned to send the Continental troops southward to reinforce Greene in South Carolina, but a shortage of clothing delayed their departure.

General Steuben first learned of the enemy's approach in the predawn hours of June 4. Two enemy detachments (one inaccurately reported to be one thousand men strong) were heading west toward Point of Fork.[37] Realizing that the Rivanna River was fordable in several places upriver, and that his position on the point was thus vulnerable to attack from these detachments, Steuben ordered the troops and military stores at Point of Fork removed to the southern bank of the deeper and wider Fluvanna (James) River. A picket of fifty men remained on the point of land between the two rivers, and a small party of dragoons was sent up the road from the point about two miles to reconnoitre.[38] These dragoons, as well as one of Steuben's mounted aides-de-camp, who had returned to the point at mid-morning to recall the picket, were promptly captured by Simcoe's advance guard. Informed by the captives that most of the military stores and troops had already been removed across the river, Simcoe pressed forward to investigate. He recalled, "The cavalry immediately advanced, and the enemy being plainly seen on the opposite side, nothing remained but to stop some boats, which were putting off from the extreme point; this Capt. Shank effected, and took about thirty people who were on the banks, from which the embarkation had proceeded."[39]

With the bulk of his troops and supplies safely across the Fluvanna (James) River, Steuben faced a tough decision: should he hold his position and try to repulse the enemy if they attempted to cross the river, or should he withdraw to the south, taking what supplies he could but leaving the rest behind? For the moment, Steuben held his ground. Across the river, Simcoe took measures to convince the general to withdraw.

Aware that his detachment was outnumbered by Steuben's force, Simcoe engaged in deception to convince the Prussian commander to withdraw from the river. Simcoe recalled,

> Every method was now taken to persuade the enemy, that [his detachment] was Earl Cornwallis's army, that they might leave the opposite shore, which was covered with arms and stores: Capt. Hutchinson with the 71st regiment, (clothed in red,) was directed to advance as near to the banks of the Fluvanna as he could . . . the baggage and women halted among the woods, on the summit of the hill, and, in that position, made the appearance of a numerous corps: the three-pounder was carried down, the artillery men being positively ordered to fire but one shot and. . . . The troops occupied the heights which covered the neck of the point, and their numbers were concealed in the wood.[40]

General Steuben (who was deployed with the bulk of his troops atop a ridge overlooking the river) was undoubtedly discouraged to learn that a single cannon shot from the enemy had scattered a fifty-man detachment posted below the ridge at the boat landing. He noted that it was only through "much persuasion and many threats," that the rattled Virginians returned to their post.[41]

As night fell, Lieutenant Colonel Simcoe developed his own concern, admitting that he was "apprehensive lest Baron Steuben, having secured his stores of which were of great value, over a broad and unfordable river, and being in possession of all the boats, should repass his troops in the night, higher up the river, and fall on him, so that, if the British troops should be beaten, they would have no retreat, being shut up between two rivers [the Fluvanna and Rivanna]."[42]

In other words, Simcoe worried that Steuben might turn the tables on Simcoe and cross the Fluvanna River above the point and trap Simcoe's smaller force on the point between the two rivers. He confessed further that he would have withdrawn his force from Point of Fork had his troops not been so fatigued from the long march there. Instead, he kept his troops on alert and hoped that his earlier deception would prevent Steuben from launching an attack.

Simcoe's efforts apparently did more than that, for around midnight his men heard the sounds of Steuben's boats being destroyed across the river.[43] Steuben had decided to withdraw under cover of darkness, abandoning a vast amount of military stores that included "two thousand five hundred stand of arms, a large quantity of gunpowder, case shot, &ct., several casks of saltpeter, sulphur, and brimstone, and upwards of sixty hogsheads of rum and brandy, several chests of carpenters' tools, and upwards of four hundred intrenching tools, with casks of flints, sail cloth and wagons."[44] A variety of artillery pieces were also abandoned—"all French pieces and in excellent order," noted Simcoe.[45]

As General Steuben fled south with his troops toward the Staunton River to escape the reach of Simcoe, Tarleton and Cornwallis (who had trailed behind Simcoe with the main army) converged on Goochland County. They united just a few miles downriver from Point of Fork at Thomas Jefferson's Elk Hill Plantation. Cornwallis rested his army and used Jefferson's house as his headquarters. He did nothing to stop his troops from plundering the estate and several neighboring properties; Elk Hill, according to its owner, was soon reduced to "an absolute waste."[46]

While Cornwallis and his five-thousand-man army enjoyed the offerings of Jefferson's property, Lafayette cautiously marched southwestward from the Rapidan River through Orange and Louisa Counties. General Anthony Wayne had still not joined Lafayette, but the Pennsylvanians were only a few days behind, and finally caught up with Lafayette at Boswell's Tavern near the South Anna River on June 10. Wayne's eight hundred Continental reinforcements emboldened Lafayette to move even closer to Cornwallis. On June 13, the young French commander informed Steuben that "we Have Again got Between the Ennemy and our [remaining] Stores."[47] Lafayette ordered Steuben to proceed northward with the Continental levies to reinforce him. General Greene would have to wait.

At Elk Hill, Cornwallis learned that the bulk of the remaining American military stores in the area had been moved farther west, out of reach. Concluding on June 13 that there was little else to accomplish west of Richmond, Cornwallis headed east toward the capital. It was also time to see if instructions from General Clinton had arrived from New York.

Lafayette cautiously trailed Cornwallis, encouraged by the addition of hundreds of riflemen under General William Campbell. On the same day that Cornwallis entered Richmond, Lafayette wrote a candid letter to his friend, the Chevalier de La Luzerne. In it he subtly criticized General Wayne and not-so-subtly criticized General Steuben:

> As yet . . . [Cornwallis] has not succeeded in bringing us into an action. For a long time we had Tarleton entering our camp two hours after it was abandoned. There was not a shot fired, and the junction with the Pennsylvanians was made. I expected that the junction would be made sooner. I expected they would be more numerous. I expected that 500 regular troops and a corps of militia attacked by 400 men, 200 of whom were armed with swords, would prevent their crossing an impassable river.[48]

Lafayette continued with a description of his own actions:

After having slipped rather fortunately between the enemy army and our stores, we made a junction with a few riflemen. Lord Cornwallis seemed not to like these hilly terrains and withdrew towards Richmond. We make it seem we are pursuing him, and my riflemen, their faces smeared with charcoal, make the woods resound with their yells; I have made them an army of devils and have given them plenary absolution. What regular troops I have are very good but few in number.[49]

Lafayette's effective Continentals (his light troops and Wayne's men) now numbered approximately 1,600 men from New England and Pennsylvania. Wayne commanded these troops, which Lafayette described as his first line. Lafayette's second line was comprised of Virginia militia, whose numbers fluctuated greatly but averaged between 1,500 to 2,000 men. Virginia's new governor, Thomas Nelson Jr. of Yorktown, commanded these troops. Another Virginia general, Peter Muhlenberg, was placed in charge of the riflemen and a detachment of light infantry. General George Weedon commanded a small party of militia in Fredericksburg, and Steuben led his force of approximately five hundred Continental recruits north from the Staunton River to reinforce Lafayette. Altogether, Lafayette commanded (directly or indirectly) approximately 4,500 troops, and although this approached the number Cornwallis had in the field, the caliber and experience of Cornwallis's troops far surpassed that of Lafayette's men. As a result, the French general remained cautious in his "pursuit."[50]

Seven

Spencer's Ordinary and Green Spring

JUNE–JULY 1781

ENERAL CORNWALLIS OCCUPIED RICHMOND FOR NEARLY A
week in mid-June, then marched east to Williamsburg, which
he entered on June 25. Lieutenant Colonel Tarleton commanded the
rear guard of the British army and trailed the column, while Lieutenant Colonel Simcoe and his detachment broke from the column
on June 22 and marched north towards Newcastle to screen the
army's left flank and draw Lafayette's attention in that direction. The
next day, June 23, Simcoe was ordered to march along the Chickahominy River and destroy whatever boats were discovered. He was
also instructed to spend a day or two collecting cattle for the army
in Williamsburg.[1]

On the same day that Cornwallis's army reached Williamsburg
(June 25), Simcoe halted twenty miles away at Cooper's Mills. Sim-
coe was anxious about the whereabouts of Lafayette's army. With
Cornwallis and the main British army a day's march away, Simcoe
worried that his detachment was vulnerable to a sudden strike by
Lafayette's much larger force. If Lafayette managed to catch Simcoe's

detachment before Simcoe closed the gap with Cornwallis, it was unlikely help from Williamsburg could arrive in time to prevent disaster.

Simcoe's concern prompted him to resume his march toward Williamsburg at 2 A.M.; he sent his infantry (two hundred Queen's Rangers and detachments of jaeger and loyalist riflemen) with his lone cannon down the Williamsburg road under Major Armstrong ahead of his cavalry (a hundred strong) and cattle. Simcoe ordered Armstrong to proceed as far as Spencer's Ordinary—a roadside tavern about fourteen miles from Cooper's Mills and only six miles northwest of Williamsburg—and wait there for the cavalry and cattle to catch up. Simcoe and his cavalry remained at Cooper's Mills with the cattle drivers (North Carolina loyalist militia), and waited for enough light to move the cattle that had been collected. They proceeded toward Spencer's Ordinary around 3 A.M.

Simcoe's infantry, which reached Spencer's Ordinary ahead of the cavalry, was resting in platoons along the road to Williamsburg when the cavalry and cattle arrived a few hours after dawn. An impatient Captain Johann Ewald (who had recovered from his wound at Scott's Creek and rejoined his jaeger company) requested permission to resume the march to Williamsburg to avoid the oppressive midday summer heat, but Simcoe decided to rest his cavalry and collect more cattle from the area before his entire detachment proceeded on to Williamsburg.[2] While a party of loyalists searched for cattle in the neighborhood of Spencer's Ordinary, Simcoe's cavalry dismounted to feed and water their horses at a nearby farm. The infantry continued to rest along the road and finished breakfast.

Unbeknownst to Simcoe, a large American detachment under Colonel Richard Butler of Pennsylvania had marched all night in pursuit. Butler's force included a regiment of Pennsylvania Continentals and two contingents of Virginia riflemen. These foot soldiers trailed behind fifty dragoons under Major William McPherson, who, "having taken up fifty light infantry behind fifty dragoons, overtook Simcoe, and regardless of numbers made an immediate charge," soon after Simcoe's cavalry halted.[3] McPherson's horses, each carrying a dragoon and a light infantryman, first encountered the Tories from North Carolina who were foraging for more cattle. They fled toward Simcoe's dismounted cavalry, abandoning the new cattle they had just collected. A lone trumpeter posted between the foragers, and the dismounted cavalry alerted Simcoe's horsemen of the enemy's approach, calling out: "draw your swords Rangers, the rebels are coming!"[4] The young trumpeter drew the charging American dragoons away from his dismounted comrades in an effort to give them time to remount their horses. The ploy worked so well that the charging Americans, who veered to the right in pursuit of the trumpeter, exposed their left flank to Simcoe's horsemen. Simcoe proudly recalled that his cavalry commander, Captain Shank, "led [his horsemen] to the charge on the enemy's flank, which was somewhat exposed . . . [and] broke them entirely."[5] The American cavalry commander was unhorsed in the melee and forced to hide in a nearby swamp until the fight concluded, and his dragoons were scattered in all directions. Fortunately for the Americans, their infantry arrived in time to take up the fight.

At the first sound of gunfire, Simcoe raced from Spencer's Ordinary, where he was meeting with Armstrong and the infantry, toward his cavalry to investigate the situation. Realizing that a strong enemy force was upon him, Simcoe ordered the baggage wagons and cattle to proceed immediately to Williamsburg. He also sent an express to Cornwallis, six miles away, with news of the American attack.[6]

Simcoe witnessed his cavalry repulse the American horsemen, but in their pursuit of the vanquished Americans, Simcoe's cavalrymen rode into the fire of American infantry deployed in a thick wood. Simcoe's startled horsemen disengaged and withdrew out of range of the Americans, at which point Simcoe joined them.[7]

While Simcoe worked to reorganize his cavalry, Ewald took charge of the infantry at Spencer's Ordinary and prepared to attack the large American force of riflemen and Continental troops that was deployed in the woods. The British infantry and jaegers formed for battle in the ploughed fields and orchard north of Spencer's Ordinary, extending a battle line (with gaps between companies) from the road eastward to an orchard. Ewald's jaegers held the right flank of this line, which extended beyond the American left flank. Ewald immediately saw an opportunity to exploit this situation, and ordered his jaegers to circle around the American left flank to attack them from the side and rear while the rest of Simcoe's infantry held the enemy's attention with a direct frontal assault.[8] Ewald personally led this assault and recalled that

> I called to Lieutenant Bickell to . . . fall upon the enemy's left flank and rear with all the jagers. At that instant, I jumped off my horse and placed myself in front of the center of the grenadiers and light infantry company. I asked them not to fire a shot, but to attack with the bayonet . . . The enemy, who had moved forward, was taken aback by our advance. [They] waited for us up to forty paces, fired a volley, killed two thirds of the grenadiers, and withdrew . . . We came among them and engaged them hand to hand. The enemy now came under rifle fire from the jagers on his flank and rear, and hurried to escape. We captured a French officer, a captain of riflemen, and twenty-two men, partly from the so-called Wild Irish Riflemen, and partly from the light infantry.[9]

As Ewald and the bulk of Simcoe's infantry advanced directly at the Americans, they were suddenly attacked on their left flank by a detachment of rebels from across the road. This force, which was separated from the rest of the American line by the fenced road that bisected the rebel line, had wheeled left to blast the left flank of Simcoe's advancing infantry. To get in position, though, the Americans had to scale two high, sturdy fences that bordered both sides of the road, and as they climbed over them they became disordered. It was at this moment that Simcoe struck with his cavalry, leading his horsemen in a charge down the road and amongst the disordered Americans. Simcoe recalled that "[the rebels] did not observe the cavalry, which while they were in this disorder, lost not the moment, but . . . charged them up the road, and upon its left, entirely broke and totally dispersed them."[10]

While Simcoe neutralized this American threat to Ewald's left flank, the bold German officer continued forward, pushing the American infantry back into the woods. He recalled that "after I had advanced several hundred paces into the wood, I halted and reformed the remainder of the three ranger companies, which did not number sixty men. We fell in on a footpath which ran through a thick brushwood."[11]

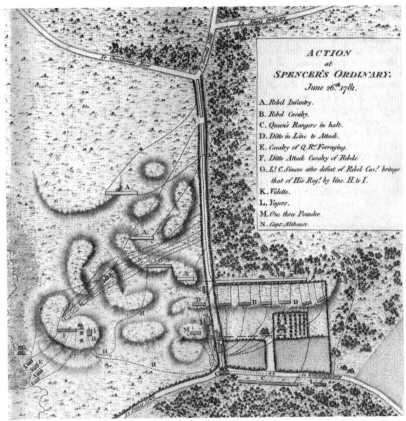

"Action at Spencer's Ordinary [Tavern]: June 26, 1781," from John Grave Simcoe's journal of the operations of the Queen's Rangers, 1787. Continental colonel Richard Butler's infantry and cavalry forces (labeled "A"center left) surprised the Queen's Rangers under the command of John Grave Simcoe (labeled "C" at the bottom, and "D" as they formed a line against the Americans); Butler's forces to the left on the map, however, did not account for Simcoe's cavalry (labeled "E" and "F") and were defeated. Simcoe then shored up the defense of Ewald's jaegers (labeled "L" on the right, just below the key), allowing the British forces to avoid defeat. (*Norman B. Leventhal Map Center, Boston Public Library*)

Lieutenant Bickell suddenly appeared in the woods and asked Ewald for permission to sound the call to reassemble his jaegers, many of whom were scattered throughout the woods in pursuit of fleeing rebels. Ewald did not want to reveal his position to the Americans, and denied the request—which turned out to be a very fortu-

nate decision, for a minute later Ewald learned that rebel reinforcements were approaching. The bold German officer recalled that "I
went several paces ahead on the path and suddenly ran into people.
I could not help myself and cried, 'Fire! Fire!' The rangers fired, and
a running fire broke out from the enemy's side for several minutes.
Then it was quiet again. I now observed that it was time to fall back
and signaled to the jagers and rangers."[12]

With his baggage and cattle safely en route to Williamsburg, Simcoe disengaged all of his troops and resumed his march toward
Williamsburg. As he had sent all of the baggage ahead at the start of
the engagement, there were no wagons available to transport the
wounded, so Simcoe left them behind at Spencer's Ordinary under a
flag of truce. About two miles into his march to Williamsburg, Simcoe met Cornwallis with a large reinforcement, and together they returned to Spencer's Ordinary, where they happily discovered that
their wounded had not been captured; the Americans had also withdrawn, taking their casualties but leaving the British behind.

Both sides claimed victory in the engagement. Lafayette reported
losses to Congress of nine killed, fourteen wounded, one captured,
and thirteen missing, and estimated Simcoe's losses at sixty killed and
a hundred wounded.[13] In a separate letter to Thomas Nelson of Yorktown, Lafayette also highlighted the boldness of McPherson's cavalry
and the effectiveness of the riflemen.[14]

Cornwallis estimated his losses in killed and wounded at thirty-
three, and reported to General Clinton that nearly the same number
of Americans were captured. He offered no estimate of American
killed and wounded aside from the observation that the number was
considerable.[15] Simcoe was more specific, recording in his journal
losses of eleven killed and twenty-five wounded.[16] Ewald put the
number of British killed and wounded at over sixty, and speculated
that the Americans had suffered far greater.[17]

Simcoe accompanied Cornwallis back to Williamsburg, which had
been occupied by the British for over a week. The Americans spent
that time encamped at Tyree's Plantation, a few miles from New Kent
Courthouse.

During his brief stay in Virginia's former capital, Cornwallis received two letters (written in mid-June) from Clinton in New York,
neither of which pleased him. The British commander in chief was

concerned about a possible French-American offensive against New York, and was eager to concentrate his forces to repulse the expected attack. Clinton instructed Cornwallis to establish a defensive post in a healthy location in Virginia (he suggested Williamsburg or Yorktown), retain the troops needed to defend the post, and send the remainder of his force to New York via transport ships.[18] Cornwallis's view that Virginia was the key to success in the South was thus dismissed by Clinton.

A frustrated Cornwallis replied to Clinton on June 30, insisting that "until Virginia was to a degree [subjugated] we could not reduce N. Carolina or have any certain hold of the back country of S. Carolina."[19] Cornwallis added that the departure of a significant portion of his troops to New York would leave him too weak to adequately defend Yorktown (which Clinton wanted to utilize as a port for the navy). Cornwallis further questioned, prophetically, "whether it is worthwhile to hold a sickly defensive post in this bay which will always be exposed to a sudden French attack."[20] Cornwallis clearly did not agree with his commander's decision to limit activities in Virginia to defensive measures, yet as he replied to Clinton he made preparations to cross the James River and march to Portsmouth to rendezvous with the British navy and comply with Clinton's instructions.

ON JULY 4, Cornwallis led his army out of Williamsburg and marched ten miles to Jamestown to cross the James River. Before he crossed the river, however, Cornwallis tried to lure Lafayette into one last engagement. Sending the Queen's Rangers across the river with the army's baggage on July 6, Cornwallis hid the rest of his troops along the northern shore. Pickets were placed on the road to Green Spring, a plantation two miles northeast of the river crossing. Cornwallis wanted to convince Lafayette that only the British rear guard remained on the north side of the river in hopes that the young French general would rashly attack. He instructed his pickets to draw the Americans toward Jamestown and a trap.

Lafayette's advance guard, which numbered around five hundred troops under General Anthony Wayne, cautiously marched toward Jamestown in the early afternoon and halted at Green Spring at 2 P.M.

Wayne's force consisted of Major McPherson's 50 Continental dragoons (augmented by a handful of gentlemen volunteers under Lieutenant Colonel John Mercer), a detachment of militia riflemen under Major Richard Call (about 150 strong), a 60-man light infantry detachment under Major William Galvan, the 1st Pennsylvania Regiment under Colonel Walter Stewart (250 strong), and 1 six-pound cannon.[21]

Conflicting reports on the number of British troops that had actually crossed the James River concerned Lafayette. He had no desire to risk his army in a general engagement against Cornwallis. Instead, the young French commander hoped only to strike the British rear guard as it covered Cornwallis's retreat across the river. Uncertain intelligence caused Lafayette to order the rest of his Continental troops (who had remained at Norrell's Mills and Chickahominy Church, eight miles in the rear) forward to Green Spring as a precaution. Three light infantry battalions and two Pennsylvania regiments hurried to Green Spring in the afternoon. The Virginia Continentals and militia remained farther back at Byrd's Ordinary, twelve miles away.

After an hour's pause at Green Spring, still unsure what enemy force lay to his front but determined to strike at Cornwallis in some way, Lafayette ordered Wayne to advance with his troops toward the ferry at Jamestown. Led by a small party of volunteer horsemen under Lieutenant Colonel Mercer and Major Call's riflemen (who fanned out in skirmish order and slowly advanced along both sides of the road to Jamestown), Wayne's troops cautiously crossed a causeway over a marsh and continued on through the open fields of Green Spring Plantation.

About half a mile into the march the road entered a long stretch of woods. Waiting in the woods were small parties of British skirmishers with orders to strongly resist the rebel advance, yet fall back when pushed. Cornwallis believed that such a show of resistance would convince the Americans that they were indeed confronting the British rear guard, and thus the rebels would push on into the trap Cornwallis had set. He explained his thinking to Clinton after the battle: "Concluding that the enemy would not bring a considerable force within our reach, unless they supposed that nothing was left but a rear guard, I took every means to convince them of my weakness, and suffered my pickets to be insulted and driven back."[22]

Cornwallis's pickets (largely selected from the 76th and 80th Regiments) waged a spirited two-hour skirmish in the woods against the American riflemen, grudgingly yielding ground under the "galling" and steady fire of the rebel riflemen. An officer of the 76th Regiment recalled that the rebels

> first began by attacking a small picquet consisting of twenty Highlanders of the 76th, commanded by Lieut. Balvaird of the 80th, who being early wounded, Lieut. Alston of the same regiment, who was accidently there, took the command of the picquet, he was also wounded. Lieut. Wemys, who was acting as adjutant to the 76th, being sent on a message to the picquet, seeing Alston wounded, dismounted and gave him his horse, drew his sword, and took command of the picquet. He had hardly had two minutes when he was wounded, and though half of the men were by this time killed or wounded the rest of the brave Highlanders kept their ground . . . till ordered in by Lord Cornwallis, but not before they had expended about 50 rounds each man.[23]

The British pickets—whose determined resistance and lack of reinforcement suggested to Wayne that his riflemen were indeed engaged with the rear guard of Cornwallis's army—eventually withdrew from the woods. They hurried across an open field and redeployed among some farm buildings and fences facing the American advance.

Lieutenant Colonel Mercer, who in the middle of the fight in the woods was called away from his horsemen on the road and ordered to command the American riflemen on the right flank, joined the riflemen at the edge of John Harris's farm. He recalled, "I found the Riflemen advanc'd near the edge of the wood [four hundred yards southwest of the road] & firing at long shot on the sentinels of a Pickett paraded before a small clapboard house."[24]

Riflemen on Wayne's left flank under Major Call and Major McPherson positioned themselves similarly in the woods at the edge of a field, and fired at British pickets positioned at William Wilkinson's farm. Call and McPherson initially did not notice the main British force, which was waiting in two lines about half a mile to the southeast to ambush the Americans, because the lay of the land and woods obscured their view. Mercer noticed them from his position on the right flank, however, and recalled that "the horse of Tarleton were form'd, at the respectable distance of four or five hundred yards; their left flank was protected by a skirt of woods, in front of which was form'd a Pickett of 100 or 150 men, beyond this on the right of Tarleton, & across the main road & in front of the church appeared, indistinctly, the main body of the British army."[25]

Thousands of British troops stood in two lines on the opposite side of John Harris's farm field and across the road to Jamestown, waiting to join the battle. Lieutenant Colonel Thomas Dundas commanded the left wing of Cornwallis's first line, which included the 43rd, 76th, and 80th Regiments with two six-pound cannon and Tarleton's Legion. The much smaller right wing of the line consisted of two battalions of light infantry under Lieutenant Colonel John Yorke. The Brigade of Guards, 23rd and 33rd Regiments, and the Prince Hereditaire Hessian Regiment made up a second line.

Wayne's advance guard was about to fall into a trap, and Lafayette, who had ridden a few miles upriver to gain a better look at the British crossings, discovered the trap just before it was sprung. Lafayette dashed back to Green Spring to recall Wayne, but it was too late; Wayne's troops were too far advanced. All Lafayette could do was deploy his last two light-infantry battalions (which had just arrived at Green Spring) to cover Wayne's inevitable retreat. Lafayette then rode forward to join Wayne. A battalion of light infantry under Major John Wyllys and the 2nd and 3rd Pennsylvania Regiments had already gone ahead in Lafayette's absence to reinforce Wayne.

While Lafayette and the reinforcements hurried forward to join the battle, Mercer and the riflemen on the American right flank concentrated on driving the British pickets from John Harris's clapboard house and farm. Mercer described what happened:

> The [enemy] Picket was speedily driven [from the house] with loss, & possession gain'd of the house. To support them

A French map of the Battle of Green Spring, published in 1781. Green Spring
plantation is at the top left center. Under the command of Gen. LaFayette, Gen.
Anthony Wayne led what he thought would be a surprise attack (labeled "C"
and "D" at the center) against Cornwallis's rear guard as his army prepared to
cross the James River at Jamestown. Instead, Cornwallis had anticipated such
a move and nearly enveloped Wayne's forces. Rather than pursue Wayne and
LaFayette, Cornwallis resumed his army's river crossing. (*Library of Congress*)

& regain the house, [a second British detachment] advanc'd with spirit, but they were unable to stand the deadly fire of the Riflemen, and were driven back with . . . loss. . . . The Riflemen embolden'd by this success, were with difficulty restrain'd from advancing . . . and a number of them crowded into the house and began to fire to the left on the main body of the British army now plainly discover'd at a distance of about 300 yards.[26]

Mercer noted that the rifle fire from the house drew the attention of British artillerists, who

open'd 3 pieces of artillery on us, at from three to four hundred yards. Almost at the first discharge my horse received a cannon ball in his body, which carried away my stirrups & bruis'd my foot . . . the shot passing through the clapboard house alarming the Riflemen within so much that they fled instantly with great trepidation; by this time I had mounted another horse, but it was impossible to rally those who had fled or stop those advanced into the field, who dispers'd in great confusion.[27]

When a report reached Wayne (who was still advancing up the road toward Cornwallis's hidden troops with the bulk of the advance guard) that a lone British cannon was struggling to withdraw on the American right, Major William Galvan requested permission to seize it. Wayne acquiesced, and Galvan reported that

I moved [with approximately 60 troops] towards the place where the [cannon reportedly was]: we soon came up with several parties of the riflemen from which I could learn nothing of the pretended retreating field piece . . . I kept moving forward and met Col. Mercer whose horse had been killed and who, wounded himself, had the gallantry to guide my little column till we came in full sight of the British line.[28]

Undoubtedly taken aback by the number of enemy troops to his front, Galvan noticed that the enemy line extended as far as he could see to his right [Cornwallis's left] but that the end of Cornwallis's right flank was obscured by woods. Wrongly assuming that it did not extend very far beyond the woods, Galvan decided to attempt to turn Cornwallis's right flank. He recalled that "I therefore wheeled to the left and soon came to a large open field, where I perceived them drawn up and stretching out of my sight with a field piece opposite to me which had already begun to play. In this critical situation, a retreat, when so far from the American line and only within 300 yards of the British was excessively dangerous."[29]

Expecting to be reinforced at any moment by Major Wyllys's light-infantry battalion, Galvan chose to fight. He moved his men (under heavy fire) across the front of the British line to a skirt of woods on his left, then wheeled right to face the enemy and commenced a "smart, running fire," just sixty yards from the foe.[30] Galvan, unaware that Wyllys's battalion had become heavily engaged on Galvan's right against the advancing British line, declared that his men fought the whole British line alone for fifteen minutes before they were nearly enveloped and forced to retire.[31] Other witnesses remember a shorter stand, but whatever the length of time, Galvan's fight was a bold display of determination and bravery.

On their way to the rear, Galvan and his men encountered Wayne, now fully aware of Cornwallis's trap. The two detachments from the 2nd and 3rd Pennsylvania Regiments had arrived in time to support the First Pennsylvanians (who had not yet engaged in the fight), and Wayne, whose flanks and front were being pressed, boldly ordered his vastly outnumbered troops to form into lines of battle and advance. In a letter to General Washington after the engagement, Wayne justified his decision to attack rather than retreat. "It was determined among a choice of difficulties, to advance and charge them. This was done with such vivacity as to produce the desired effect, that is, checking them in their advance, and diverting them from their [attempted encirclement]."[32]

Lieutenant William Feltman of the 1st Pennsylvania Regiment described the advance:

We . . . displayed to the right and left, the 3rd battalion on our right, and the 2nd on our left, being then formed, [we] brought on a general engagement, our advance [was] regular at a charge till we got within eighty yards of their whole army, they being regularly formed, standing one yard distance from each other . . . We advanced under a heavy fire of grape-shot at which distance we opened our musketry.[33]

Ensign Ebenezer Denny, who was also in the center of Wayne's line with the 1st Pennsylvania Regiment, was thrust in charge of his company after his captain was wounded. Denny candidly described the experience in his journal. "Young and inexperienced, exhausted with hunger and fatigue, had like to have disgraced myself— had eat nothing all day but a few blackberries—was faint, and with difficulty kept my place; once or twice was about to throw away my arms (a very heavy espontoon)." [34] Denny continued, "We could not have been engaged longer than about three or four minutes, but at a distance of sixty yards only."[35]

All who participated or witnessed the engagement noted the intensity of those few minutes of Wayne's advance. British lieutenant colonel Banastre Tarleton actually complimented the American Continentals for their gallantry: "The conflict in this quarter was severe and well contested. The artillery and infantry of each army . . . were for some minutes warmly engaged not fifty yards asunder . . . on the left of the British, the action was for some time gallantly maintained by the Continental infantry."[36]

Major Galvan, who managed to redeploy his detachment on the left of the Pennsylvania line and join Wayne's advance, recalled that the American line marched forward about thirty yards, which prompted the British to halt their advance and pour "an immense fire upon us."[37] Wayne's bold movement had momentarily frozen Cornwallis's troops, but the Pennsylvanians soon halted too. Galvan noted that

our stop encouraged the British and, tho' our fire was as brisk as could be expected from so small a line, they began to move rapidly upon us and the right of the Pennsylvanians to give way, the left followed, and the enemy making a devil of a noise of firing and huzzaing [cheering] (tho' by the by they did not push on very fast) all on our side became a scene of confusion.[38]

Wayne, realizing that the confusion caused by his unexpected advance had subsided among the British, ordered a retreat. He explained to Washington that, "being employed by numbers [vastly greater than his, and with] many brave and worthy officers and soldiers killed or wounded, we found it expedient to fall back half a mile to Green Spring Farm."[39]

Luckily for the Americans, the lateness of the day prevented an aggressive pursuit by Cornwallis, much to the displeasure of some of his subordinates. A Pennsylvania newspaper printed an excerpt of a letter from an American officer, who claimed "the British officers we are informed, are much displeased at [the outcome of the battle] and acknowledge they were outgeneraled; otherwise they must have cut to pieces our small detachment, aided as they were by 500 horse, and a considerable body of their infantry mounted."[40]

The American officer went on to defend Wayne's bold decision to attack:

> We could not possibly have extricated ourselves from the difficulties we were in but by the manouvre we adopted, which although it may have the appearance of temerity to those unacquainted with circumstances, yet was founded upon the truest military principles: And was one of those necessary, though daring measures, which seldom fail of producing the desired effect, that is, confusing the enemy and opening a way to retreat in sight of a much superior army.[41]

Although the Battle of Green Spring was a British victory, American losses (which were roughly double the seventy men Cornwallis lost), could have been far worse.[42] In that sense, Green Spring was a missed opportunity for the British.

IN THE DAYS FOLLOWING the Battle of Green Spring, Cornwallis completed his movement across the James River, informed Clinton in New York that the troops Clinton requested from Virginia would soon depart from Portsmouth (most never sailed), and ordered Tarleton to raid Prince Edward Courthouse and New London (in Bedford County) far to the west. Tarleton was instructed to "do everything in your power to destroy the supplies destined for the rebel army."[43] This included "all public stores of corn and provisions."[44] Cornwallis added, "If there should be a quantity of provisions or corn collected at a private house, I would have you destroy it, even [if] there should be no proof of its being intended for the public service, leaving enough for the support of the family, as there is the greatest reason to apprehend that such provisions will be ultimately appropriated by the enemy to the use of General Greene's army."[45]

Across the James River, Lafayette misinterpreted reports of Tarleton's movement westward to mean that Cornwallis was heading back to the Carolinas. Further reports correctly indicated that only part of the British army had marched toward Petersburg; the rest headed south toward Portsmouth. Unsure what Cornwallis was up to, Lafayette split his army; Wayne led approximately five hundred Pennsylvanian and four hundred Virginian Continentals across the James River, then westward to Goode's Bridge in Amelia County, to be in position to strike Tarleton on his return or follow Tarleton southward if his destination was the Carolinas.[46]

While Wayne camped at Goode's Bridge, Tarleton completed a two week, four-hundred-mile circuit of south-central Virginia and returned to Portsmouth without incident, upset that "the stores destroyed . . . were not in quantity or value equivalent to the damage sustained in the skirmishes on the route, and the loss of men and horses by the excessive heat of the climate."[47]

Lafayette and the rest of the American army in Virginia (the light-infantry corps and militia) spent most of July a few miles below Richmond at Malvern Hill, where they waited for Cornwallis's intentions to become clear. Lafayette's encampment sat on the north side of the James River and was described by the general as "the Most Airy and Healthy place this side of the Mountains."[48] Across the river and far to the south, outside of Portsmouth, Colonel Josiah Parker commanded a detachment of militia, but his numbers were too small to challenge Cornwallis in Portsmouth.

General Clinton in New York was not pleased to learn of Cornwallis's move to Portsmouth. He informed his subordinate in mid-July that "I had flattered myself [that] . . . you would, at least, have waited for a line from me . . . before you finally determined upon so serious and mortifying a move, as the re-passing James River and retiring with your army to Portsmouth."[49]

Clinton and the British navy wanted Cornwallis to establish a secure, deep-water port for the navy around Hampton or Yorktown. Clinton planned to send a large expedition up the Chesapeake Bay in the fall, and desired a staging area other than Portsmouth (which he thought was too sickly and confined for the navy) to launch it from. Additionally, the British navy desired a safe location for part of its fleet to spend the winter. Clinton preferred Old Point Comfort near Hampton or Yorktown, which sat on the York River and looked out onto Chesapeake Bay. Clinton left the final choice of a site to Cornwallis, and instructed him to retain whatever troops necessary to properly defend the post.[50] To comply with Clinton's wishes, Cornwallis retained most of the troops that were about to embark for New York and made preparations to abandon Portsmouth. Yorktown was his destination.

The first British troops landed in Yorktown at the beginning of August, and for the next three weeks Cornwallis and his army worked to dismantle their defenses at Portsmouth and erect new ones at Yorktown and Gloucester Point, directly across the York River from Yorktown. They had no way to know that before they completed this task Washington, in New York with the main American army, set in motion a plan to trap Cornwallis in Yorktown. Supported by the surprise arrival in the Chesapeake Bay of a powerful French fleet, which drove off the British navy in early September and cut British support for Cornwallis by sea, Washington rushed both American and French reinforcements from the north to Virginia to encircle and besiege Lord Cornwallis. These troops, in combination with the troops in Virginia under General Lafayette, surpassed twenty thousand strong, and descended on the British position at Yorktown in late September. The last great battle of the Revolutionary War, the Siege of Yorktown, had begun.

NOTES

CHAPTER ONE: "TO MAKE A SOLID MOVE INTO NORTH CAROLINA"

1. An embarkation list prepared by Hessian major Carl Baurmeister notes that General Clinton brought approximately 8,700 men with him for the siege of Charleston. Clinton estimates that he returned to New York in June 1780 with 4,500 men. Bernard Uhlendorf, trans. and ed., *The Siege of Charleston with an Account of the Province of South Carolina: Diaries and Letters of Hessian Officers from the von Jungkenn Papers in the William L. Clements Library*, vol. 12 (Ann Arbor: University of Michigan Press, 1938), 108–9; William Willcox, ed., *The American Rebellion: Sir Henry Clinton's Narrative of His Campaigns, 1775–1782, with an Appendix of Original Documents* (London: Oxford University Press, 1954), 191n6.

2. Willcox, ed., 186.

3. K. G. Davies, ed., "Major-General Leslie to Lord George Germain, November 27, 1780," *Documents of the American Revolution*, vol. 18 (Shannon: Irish University Press, 1978), 235; Lieut. Col. Banastre Tarleton, *A History of the Campaigns of 1780 and 1781 in the Southern Provinces of North America* (North Stratford, NH: Ayer Co., 1999), 158–59.

4. Lyman C. Draper, *King's Mountain and Its Heroes: History of the Battle of King's Mountain* (Cincinnati: Peter G. Thomson, 1881), 169.

5. Draper, "*Virginia Gazette*, November 11, 1780," *King's Mountain and Its Heroes*, 204.

6. Tarleton, "Extract of a letter from Major Ferguson to Lord Cornwallis, published by the Americans," *A History of the Campaigns of 1780 and 1781 in the Southern Provinces of North America* (1787; North Stratford, NH: Ayer Co., 1999), 193.

7. Mark M. Boatner III, *Encyclopedia of the American Revolution* (Stackpole Books, 1966), 579.

8. Patrick O'Kelly, *Nothing but Blood and Slaughter: The Revolutionary War in the Carolinas*, vol. 2 (Lillington, NC: Blue House Tavern Press, 2004), 322–25.

9. Draper, "Colonel Isaac Shelby's Account of King's Mountain," *King's Mountain and Its Heroes*, 543.

10. Draper, "Col. Wm. Campbell to Col. Arthur Campbell, October 20, 1780," *King's Mountain and Its Heroes*, 526.

11. Draper, *King's Mountain and Its Heroes*, 247.

12. Draper, "Colonel Isaac Shelby's Account of King's Mountain," *King's Mountain and Its Heroes*, 543.

13. John M. Roberts, ed., *Autobiography of a Revolutionary Soldier* (1859; New York: Arno Press, 1979), 52.

14. "Kings Mountain Expedition," *An Annual Publication of Historical Papers: Governor W. W. Holden and Revolutionary Documents*, Third Series (Durham, NC: Historical Society of Trinity College, 1899), 85.

15. Draper, *Kings Mountain and Its Heroes*, 249.

16. George Scheer and Hugh Rankin, *Rebels and Redcoats: The American Revolution Through the Eyes of Those Who Fought and Lived It* (New York: Da Capo Press, 1957), 418.

17. E. Alfred Jones, ed., *The Journal of Alexander Chesney, A South Carolina Loyalist in the Revolution and After*, printed from a copy at the Ohio State Library (1921), 17–18.

18. Draper, *King's Mountain and Its Heroes*, 543.

19. Willcox, ed., "General Clinton to General Leslie, October 12, 1780," *The American Rebellion: Sir Henry Clinton's Narratives of his Campaigns*, 467.

20. Ibid.

21. Julian P. Boyd, ed. "Thomas Jefferson to Samuel Huntington, November 3, 1780," *The Papers of Thomas Jefferson*, vol. 4 (Princeton, NJ: Princeton University Press, 1951), 92.

22. Willcox, ed., *The American Rebellion: Sir Henry Clinton's Narrative of His Campaigns*, 231

23. Davies, ed., "Major-General Leslie to Lord George Germain, November 27, 1780," *Documents of the American Revolution*, vol. 18, 235.

24. Boyd ed., "Thomas Jefferson to Samuel Huntington, October 25, 1780," *The Papers of Thomas Jefferson*, vol. 4.

25. Davies, ed., "Major-General Alexander Leslie to Lord George Germain, November 27, 1780," *Documents of the American Revolution*, vol. 18, 235.

26. Willcox, ed., " General Leslie, to General Clinton, November 4, 1780," *The American Rebellion: Sir Henry Clinton's Narrative of His Campaigns*, 472–73.

27. Ibid.

28. Boyd, ed., "Thomas Jefferson to Samuel Huntington, November 3, 1780," *The Papers of Thomas Jefferson*, vol. 4, 92–93.

29. Ibid.

CHAPTER TWO: BENEDICT ARNOLD INVADES VIRGINIA

1. Willcox, ed., *The American Rebellion: Sir Henry Clinton's Narrative of His Campaigns*, 234.

2. Willcox, ed., *The American Rebellion: Sir Henry Clinton's Narrative of His Campaigns*, 235.

3. Davies, ed., "General Henry Clinton to General Arnold, December 14, 1780," *Documents of the American Revolution*, vol. 18, 256.

4. Joseph Tustin, ed., *Diary of the American War: A Hessian Journal* (New Haven: Yale University Press, 1979), 258. Henceforth referred to as Ewald and Davies, eds., "Disposition of H. M. Ships, July 4, 1781," *Documents of the American Revolution*, vol. 20, 173.

5. "Embarkation Return for the Following Corps, December 11, 1780, New

York," *Sir Henry Clinton Papers*, 113:15, University of Michigan, William L. Clements Library.

6. Ibid.

7. Boyd, ed., "Governor Jefferson to General Steuben, December 31, 1781," *The Papers of Thomas Jefferson*, vol. 4, 254.

8. John K. Laughton, ed., *The Journal of Rear-Admiral Bartholomew James* (London: Navy Records Society, 1896), 94. Henceforth referred to as "Bartholomew James Journal."

9. Ibid.

10. Ibid.

11. Ibid., 95.

12. "Extract of a letter from a Gentleman in Portsmouth, Virginia, to his Friend in this city, dated January 24, 1781," *New York Gazette and Weekly Mercury*, February 5, 1781.

13. Bartholomew James Journal, 96.

14. Ewald, *Diary of the American War: A Hessian Journal*, 259.

15. Ibid.

16. Ibid.

17. Ibid.

18. Ibid.

19. Ibid.

20. Ibid.

21. Ibid., 260.

22. Ibid., 259–60.

23. Ibid., 260.

24. Michael Kranish, *Flight from Monticello: Thomas Jefferson at War* (Oxford: Oxford University Press, 2010), 172.

25. Bartholomew James Journal, 100.

26. Davies, ed., "General Arnold to General Clinton, January 21, 1781," *Documents of the American Revolution*, vol. 20, 40.

27. Boyd, ed., "William Tatham to William Armistead Burwell, June 13, 1805," *The Papers of Thomas Jefferson*, vol. 4, 274.

28. Boyd, ed., "Nathaniel Burwell to Governor Jefferson, January 2, 1781," *The Papers of Thomas Jefferson*, vol. 4, 294.

29. Kranish, "General Arnold to the Officer Commanding the Party on Shore, January 2, 1781," *Flight from Monticello*, 173.

30. Ibid.

31. Ewald, *Diary of the American War: A Hessian Journal*, 260–61.

32. Ibid.

33. Boyd, ed., "Governor Jefferson to General Nelson, January 2, 1781," *The Papers of Thomas Jefferson*, vol. 4, 297.

34. Ibid.

35. Boyd, ed., "Governor Jefferson to General Steuben, January 2, 1781," *The Papers of Thomas Jefferson*, vol. 4, 298.

36. Boyd, ed., "Jefferson Diary, January 2, 1781," 258; "Governor Jefferson to Francis Taylor, January 2, 1781," *The Papers of Thomas Jefferson*, vol. 4, 299.

37. Boyd, ed., "Arnold's Invasion as Reported by Jefferson in the *Virginia Gazette*, January 13, 1781," *The Papers of Thomas Jefferson*, vol. 4, 269.

38. John G. Simcoe, *Simcoe's Military Journal: A History of the Operations of a Partisan Corps Called the Queen's Rangers* (New York: Bartlett and Welford, 1844), 159.

39. Wm. Palmer, ed., "James Cocke to Col. George Muter, January 18, 1781," *Calendar of Virginia State Papers*, vol. 1 (1875), 442.

40. Ibid.

41. Ewald, *Diary of the American War: A Hessian Journal*, 261.

42. Simcoe, *Simcoe's Military Journal*, 160.

43. Ibid.

44. Palmer, ed., "James Cocke to Col. George Muter, January 18, 1781," *Calendar of Virginia State Papers*, vol. 1, 442.

45. Ibid.

46. Davies, "General Arnold to General Clinton, January 21, 1781," *Documents of the American Revolution*, vol. 20, 40.

47. Ibid.; Ewald, *Diary of the American War: A Hessian Journal*, 261.

48. Kranish, *Flight from Monticello*, 122.

49. Simcoe, *Simcoe's Military Journal*, 161.

50. Ewald, *Diary of the American War: A Hessian Journal*, 266.

51. Boyd, ed., "Benjamin Harrison to Governor Jefferson, January 4, 1781," *The Papers of Thomas Jefferson*, vol. 4, 304.

52. Ewald, *Diary of the American War: A Hessian Journal*, 266–67.

53. Simcoe, *Simcoe's Military Journal*, 161.

54. Simcoe, *Simcoe's Military Journal*, 162.

55. Ewald, *Diary of the American War: A Hessian Journal*, 267.

56. Ibid.

57. Simcoe, *Simcoe's Military Journal*, 162.

58. Ewald, *Diary of the American War: A Hessian Journal*, 267.

59. Ibid.

60. Ibid.

61. Simcoe, *Simcoe's Military Journal*, 162.

62. Ibid.

63. Ibid.

64. Ewald, *Diary of the American War: A Hessian Journal*, 267–68.

65. Simcoe, *Simcoe's Military Journal*, 163.

66. Davies, ed., "General Arnold to General Clinton, January 21, 1781," *Documents of the American Revolution*, vol. 20, 40.

67. Ewald, *Diary of the American War: A Hessian Journal*, 268.

68. Davies, ed., "General Arnold to General Clinton, January 21, 1781," *Documents of the American Revolution*, vol. 20, 41.

69. Boyd, ed., "Jefferson Diary, January 5, 1781," *The Papers of Thomas Jefferson*, vol. 4, 259.

70. Boyd, ed., "General Steuben to Governor Jefferson, January 6, 1781," *The Papers of Thomas Jefferson*, vol. 4, 312.

71. Davies, ed., "General Arnold to General Clinton, January 21, 1781," *Documents of the American Revolution*, vol. 20, 41.

72. "Return of Ordinance, Ammunition, Stores, Small Arms, taken and destroyed at Richmond and Westham in Virginia," *Royal Georgia Gazette*, March 8, 1781, 2.

73. Ewald, *Diary of the American War: A Hessian Journal*, 268.

74. Ibid.

75. Simcoe, *Simcoe's Military Journal*, 164.

76. Ewald, *Diary of the American War: A Hessian Journal*, 268.

77. Boyd, ed., "General Nelson to Governor Jefferson, January 8, 1781," *The Papers of Thomas Jefferson*, vol. 4, 321.

78. Boyd, ed., "Governor Jefferson to General Washington, January 10, 1781," *The Papers of Thomas Jefferson*, vol. 4, 334.

79. Simcoe, *Simcoe's Military Journal*, 165.

80. Ibid., 166.

81. Ibid.

82. Ibid.

83. Ewald, *Diary of the American War: A Hessian Journal*, 269; *New York Royal Gazette*, February 7, 1781.

84. *Connecticut Journal*, February 15, 1781, 2.

85. Richard K. Showman, ed., "General Steuben to General Greene, January 11, 1781," *The Papers of Nathanael Greene*, vol. 7 (Chapel Hill: University of North Carolina Press, 1994), 98. Col. George Rogers Clark was in Richmond when Arnold arrived in Virginia and offered his services to Governor Jefferson, who accepted and sent Clark to General Steuben.

86. Davies, ed., "General Arnold to General Clinton, January 21,1781," *Documents of the American Revolution*, vol. 20, 41.

87. Simcoe, *Simcoe's Military Journal*, 168.

88. Ewald, *Diary of the American War: A Hessian Journal*, 269.

89. Ibid.

90. Ibid., 270.

91. Ibid.

92. Davies, ed., "General Arnold to General Clinton, January 21, 1781," *Documents of the American Revolution*, vol. 20, 42.

93. Ewald, *Diary of the American War: A Hessian Journal*, 270–71.

94. Davies, ed., "General Arnold to General Clinton, January 21, 1781," *Documents of the American Revolution*, vol. 20, 41.

95. *Royal Gazette*, New York, February 3, 1781, 2.

96. Ewald, *Diary of the American War: A Hessian Journal*, 271.

97. Ibid., 272.

98. Boyd, ed., "General Steuben to Governor Jefferson, January 12, 1781," *The Papers of Thomas Jefferson*, vol. 4, 345.

99. Rob Friar, *The Militia Are Coming in from All Quarters; The Revolution in Virginia's Lower Counties, 1781* (2010), 21.

100. Ewald, *Diary of the American War: A Hessian Journal*, 273.

101. Ibid.

102. Ibid.

103. Ibid.

104. Ibid.

105. Ibid.

CHAPTER THREE: A DIFFICULT WINTER FOR BOTH SIDES

1. Boyd, ed., "Nathanael Greene to Thomas Jefferson, December 6, 1780," *The Papers of Thomas Jefferson*, vol. 4, 183.

2. Henry Lee III, *The Revolutionary War Memoirs of General Henry Lee* (1812; New York : Da Capo Press, 1998), 222.

3. Lawrence E. Babits, *A Devil of a Whipping: The Battle of Cowpens* (Chapel Hill: University of North Carolina Press, 1998), 44–45.

4. Scheer and Rankin, "Account of Thomas Young," *Rebels and Redcoats*, 428.

5. Boatner III, *Encyclopedia of the American Revolution*, 293.

6. Babits, *A Devil of a Whipping*, 81.

7. Ibid.

8. Boatner III, *Encyclopedia of the American Revolution*, 293. The number of troops in the militia line has been reported as high as 1,000. See Tarleton, 216. If the bulk of the skirmish line joined the militia line, then the number would have approached 500.

9. Babits, *A Devil of a Whipping*, 41–42.

10. John Buchanan, *The Road to Guilford Courthouse: The American Revolution in the Carolinas* (New York: John Wiley and Sons, 1997), 321.

11. Scheer and Rankin, "Thomas Young," *Rebels and Redcoats*, 430.

12. Showman, ed., "General Morgan to General Greene, January 19, 1781," *The Papers of General Nathanael Greene*, vol. 7, 154.

13. Ibid., 92.

14. Showman, ed., "General Morgan to General Greene, January 19, 1781," *The Papers of General Nathanael Greene*, vol. 7, 154.

15. Tarleton, "Tarleton to Earl Cornwallis, January 4, 1781," *A History of the Campaigns of 1780 and 1781 in the Southern Provinces of North America*, 216.

16. Babits, *A Devil of a Whipping*, 103.

17. Henry Steele Commager and Richard B. Morris, eds., "Lieutenant Colonel John Eager Howard's Account," *The Spirit of Seventy-Six* (Edison, NJ: Castle Books, 2002), 1156.

18. Ibid.

19. Showman, ed., "General Morgan to General Greene, January 19, 1781," *The Papers of General Nathanael Greene*, vol. 7, 154.

20. Babits, *A Devil of a Whipping*, 117.

21. Commager and Morris, eds., "Lieutenant Colonel John Eager Howard's Account," *The Spirit of Seventy-Six*, 1156.

22. Ibid., 1157.

23. Showman, ed., "General Morgan to General Greene, January 19, 1781," *The Papers of General Nathanael Greene*, vol. 7, 154.

24. Babits, *A Devil of a Whipping*, 143.

25. Showman, ed., "General Daniel Morgan to General Nathanael Greene, January 23, 1781," *The Papers of General Nathanael Greene*, vol. 7, 178.

26. Showman, ed., "General Daniel Morgan to General Nathanael Greene, January 29, 1781," *The Papers of General Nathanael Greene*, vol. 7, 215.

27. Tarleton, "Cornwallis to Lord Germain, March 17, 1781," *A History of the Campaigns of 1780 and 1781 in the Southern Provinces of North America*, 262.

28. Showman, ed., "War Council, February 9, 1781," *The Papers of General Nathanael Greene*, vol. 7, 261.

29. Showman, ed., "General Greene to General Washington, February 9, 1781," *The Papers of General Nathanael Greene*, vol. 7, 267–69.

30. Ibid.

31. Showman, ed., "Colonel Otho Williams to General Greene, February 11, 1781," *The Papers of General Nathanael Greene*, vol. 7, 283.

32. Lawrence E. Babits and Joshua B. Howard, *Long, Obstinate, and Bloody: The Battle of Guilford Courthouse* (Chapel Hill: University of North Carolina Press, 2009), 32.

33. Lee, *The Revolutionary War Memoirs of General Henry Lee*, 240.

34. Ibid.

35. Ibid., 241.

36. Ibid., 242.

37. Ibid.

38. Ibid.

39. Ibid., 244.

40. Ibid., 238.

41. Ibid., 245.

42. Ibid.

43. Ibid.

44. Showman, ed., "Col. Otho Williams to Gen. Greene, February 13, 1781," *The Papers of General Nathanael Greene*, vol. 7, 285–86.

45. Lee, *The Revolutionary War Memoirs of General Henry Lee*, 246.

46. Tarleton, "Cornwallis to Lord Germain, March 17, 1781," *A History of the Campaigns of 1780 and 1781 in the Southern Provinces of North America*, 264.

47. Showman, ed., "Col. Otho Williams to Gen. Greene, February 14, 1781," *The Papers of General Nathanael Greene*, vol. 7, 287.

48. Lee, *The Revolutionary War Memoirs of General Henry Lee*, 247.

49. Boyd, ed., "Colonel Robert Lawson to Governor Jefferson, January 28, 1781," *The Papers of Thomas Jefferson*, vol. 4, 461.

50. Henry A. Muhlenberg, "General Muhlenberg to General Steuben, January 31, 1781," *The Life of Major-General Peter Muhlenberg* (Philadelphia: Cary and Hart, 1849), 381–82.

51. Ewald, *Diary of the American War: A Hessian Journal*, 277.

52. Ibid.

53. Ibid.

54. Ibid.

55. Ibid, 278.

56. Ibid., 279.

57. Ibid., 280.

58. Ibid., 281.

59. Ibid., 281, 284.

60. Ibid.

61. Ibid.

62. Ibid., 284.

63. Ibid., 285.

64. Ibid.

65. Muhlenberg, "General Muhlenberg to General Greene, February 24, 1781," *The Life of Major-General Peter Muhlenberg*, 388–89.

66. Friar, *The Militia Are Coming in from All Quarters*, 40. This is an account of the incident from a participant, William McLaurine of the Powhatan County militia. The full account is found in the *Virginia Magazine of History and Biography*, vol. 14, 198.

67. Muhlenberg, "General Isaac Gregory to General Muhlenberg, February 23, 1781," *The Life of Major-General Peter Muhlenberg*, 386.

68. Ewald, *Diary of the American War: A Hessian Journal*, 286.

69. Ibid.

70. Ibid.

71. Ibid.

72. Ibid., 287.

73. Muhlenberg, "General Muhlenberg to General Greene, February 24, 1781," *The Life of Major-General Peter Muhlenberg*, 389–90.

74. Boyd, ed., "General Greene to Governor Jefferson, February 15, 1781," *The Papers of Thomas Jefferson*, vol. 4, 615.

75. Showman, ed., "General Greene to General Washington, February 15, 1781," *The Papers of General Nathanael Greene*, vol. 7, 293–94.

76. Showman, ed., "General Greene to Joseph Clay, February 17, 1781," *The Papers of General Nathanael Greene*, vol. 7, 300.

77. Showman, ed., "General Greene to General Pickens, February 19, 1781," *The Papers of General Nathanael Greene*, vol. 7, 316.

CHAPTER FOUR: CORNWALLIS CATCHES GREENE

1. Showman, ed., "Lt. Col. Lee to Gen. Greene, February 20, 1781," *The Papers of General Nathanael Greene*, vol. 7, 324.

2. Showman, ed., "General Greene to General Pickens, February 21, 1781," *The Papers of General Nathanael Greene*, vol. 7, 327.

3. Tarleton, *A History of the Campaigns of 1780 and 1781 in the Southern Provinces of North America*, 231.

4. Lee, *The Revolutionary War Memoirs of General Henry Lee*, 256.

5. Ibid., 257.

6. Ibid., 258.

7. Major William Graham, "Joseph Graham to Judge Murphey, December 20, 1827," *General Joseph Graham and His Papers on North Carolina Revolutionary History* (Raleigh, NC: Edwards and Broughton, 1904), 207.

8. Graham, *General Joseph Graham and His Papers*, 319–320.

9. Showman, ed., "Lt. Col. Lee to General Greene, February 25, 1781," *The Papers of General Nathanael Greene*, vol. 7, 348.

10. Showman, ed., "General Pickens to General Greene, February 26, 1781," *The Papers of General Nathanael Greene*, vol. 7, 355.

11. Tarleton, *A History of the Campaigns of 1780 and 1781 in the Southern Provinces of North America*, 234.

12. Showman, ed., "General Greene to General Steuben, February 29, 1781," *The Papers of General Nathanael Greene*, vol. 7, 375.

13. Babits and Howard, *Long, Obstinate, and Bloody*, 43.

14. Tarleton, "Earl Cornwallis to Lord George Germain, March 17, 1781," *A History of the Campaigns of 1780 and 1781 in the Southern Provinces of North America*, 266.

15. Ibid.

16. Showman, ed., "Col. Otho Williams to General Greene, March 7, 1781," *The Papers of General Nathanael Greene*, vol. 7, 407.

17. Ibid.

18. Graham, *General Joseph Graham and His Papers*, 343.

19. Graham, *General Joseph Graham and His Papers*, 343.

20. Tarleton, "Earl Cornwallis to Lord George Germain, March 17, 1781," *A History of the Campaigns of 1780 and 1781 in the Southern Provinces of North America*, 266.

21. Tarleton, *A History of the Campaigns of 1780 and 1781 in the Southern Provinces of North America*, 238.

22. Graham, *General Joseph Graham and His Papers*, 346–47.

23. Showman, ed., "Col. Williams to General Greene, March 7, 1781," *The Papers of General Nathanael Greene*, vol. 7, 407.

24. Graham, *General Joseph Graham and His Papers*, 346.

25. Boyd, ed., "Charles Magill to Governor Jefferson, March 10, 1781," *The Papers of Thomas Jefferson*, vol. 5, 121.

26. Showman, ed., "General Greene to Colonel Henry Lee Jr., March 9, 1781," *The Papers of General Nathanael Greene*, vol. 7, 415.

27. Ibid.

28. Ibid.

29. Showman, ed., "Lt. Col. Lee to General Greene, March 11, 1781," *The Papers of General Nathanael Greene*, vol. 7, 427–28.

30. Showman, ed., "Lt. Col. Lee to General Greene, March 12, 1781," *The Papers of General Nathanael Greene*, vol. 7, 428.

31. Tarleton, "General Cornwallis to Lord Germain, March 17, 1781," *A History of the Campaigns of 1780 and 1781 in the Southern Provinces of North America*, 267.

32. Showman, ed., "General Greene to Congress, March 16, 1781," *The Papers of General Nathanael Greene*, vol. 7, 433.

33. Thomas Baker, *Another Such Victory: The Story of the American Defeat at Guilford Courthouse That Helped Win the War for Independence* (Ft. Washington, PA: Eastern National, 2005), 40–41.

34. Babits and Howard, *Long, Obstinate, and Bloody*, 51.

35. Lee, *The Revolutionary War Memoirs of General Henry Lee*, 273–74.

36. Babits and Howard, *Long, Obstinate, and Bloody*, 53.

37. Lee, *The Revolutionary War Memoirs of General Henry Lee*, 274–75.

38. Baker, *Another Such Victory*, 55.

39. Lee, *The Revolutionary War Memoirs of General Henry Lee*, 277.

40. Baker, *Another Such Victory*, 52.

41. Ibid., 56.

42. Ibid., 59.

43. Showman, ed., "General Greene to Samuel Huntington, March 16, 1781," *The Papers of General Nathanael Greene*, vol. 7, 434.

44. Roger Lamb, *An Original and Authentic Journal of Occurrences During the Late American War* (Dublin: Wilkinson and Courtney, 1809), 361.

45. Buchanan, *Road to Guilford Courthouse*, 375.

46. Ibid.

47. Tarleton, *A History of the Campaigns of 1780 and 1781 in the Southern Provinces of North America*, 273.

48. Tarleton, "Lord Cornwallis to Lord George Germain, March 17, 1781," *A History of the Campaigns of 1780 and 1781 in the Southern Provinces of North America*, 305–7.

49. Tarleton, *A History of the Campaigns of 1780 and 1781 in the Southern Provinces of North America*, 273–74.

50. C. Stedman, *The History of the Origin, Progress, and Termination of the American War*, vol. 2 (London: 1794), 339.

51. Lee, *The Revolutionary War Memoirs of General Henry Lee*, 278–79.

52. Commager and Morris, "Major St. George Tucker to his Wife, March 18, 1781," *The Spirit of Seventy-Six*, 1166.

53. Showman, ed. "General Greene to Samuel Huntington, March 16, 1781," *The Papers of General Nathanael Greene*, vol. 7, 435.

54. Boyd, ed., "General Greene to Thomas Jefferson, March 16, 1781," *The Papers of Thomas Jefferson*, vol. 5, 156.

55. Lee, *The Revolutionary War Memoirs of General Henry Lee*, 279.

56. Ibid.

57. Baker, *Another Such Victory*, 73.

58. Lamb, *An Original and Authentic Journal of Occurrences During the Late American War*, 351.

59. Baker, *Another Such Victory*, 74.

60. Ibid., 75.

61. Davies, ed., "General Earl Cornwallis to General Sir Henry Clinton, April 10, 1781," *Documents of the American Revolution*, vol. 20, 107.

62. Ibid., 108.

63. Friar, *The Militia Are Coming in from All Quarters*, 43.

64. Muhlenberg, "Colonel Parker to General Muhlenberg, March 2, 1781," *The Life of Major-General Peter Muhlenberg*, 394.

65. Ibid.

66. Ibid., 393.

67. Simcoe, *Simcoe's Military Journal*, 181.

68. Ibid.

69. Ibid., 177.

70. Ibid.

71. Ibid., 177–78.

72. Boyd, ed., *The Papers of Thomas Jefferson*, vol. 4, 294. Refers to Dixon and Hunter, *Virginia Gazette*, March 10, 1781. British military records do not corroborate the loss of any officer in this engagement.

73. Ewald, *Diary of the American War: A Hessian Journal*, 287.

74. Ibid., 288.

75. Ibid.

76. Ibid.

77. Ibid.

78. Ibid., 289. A fire ship was a vessel that, when utilized, was sailed into a formation of enemy ships and intentionally set on fire in hopes that the blaze would spread to the enemy vessels.

79. Stanley J. Idzerda, ed., "General Lafayette to General Weedon, March 20, 1781," *Lafayette in the Age of the American Revolution*, vol. 3 (Ithaca: Cornell University Press, 1980). 406.

80. Ewald, *Diary of the American War: A Hessian Journal*, 289.

81. Ibid., 290.

82. Ibid.

83. Ibid.

84. Ibid.

85. Ibid., 291.

86. Ibid.

87. Boyd, ed., "General Weedon to Governor Jefferson, March 20, 1781," *The Papers of Thomas Jefferson*, vol. 5, 185–86.

88. Boyd, ed., "James Barron to Governor Jefferson, March 21, 1781," *The Papers of Thomas Jefferson*, vol. 5, 187.

89. Boyd, ed., "Richard Barron to Governor Jefferson, March 26, 1781," *The Papers of Thomas Jefferson*, vol. 5, 238.

90. Idzerda, ed., "General Lafayette to General Washington, March 26, 1781," *Lafayette in the Age of the American Revolution*, vol. 3, 417.

CHAPTER FIVE: BRITISH OFFENSIVE OPERATIONS RESUME IN VIRGINIA

1. Davies, ed., "General Earl Cornwallis to General Henry Clinton, April 10, 1781," *Documents of the American Revolution*, vol. 20, 108.

2. Davies, ed., "General Earl Cornwallis to Lord George Germain, April 18, 1781," *Documents of the American Revolution*, vol. 20, 113.

3. Ibid.

4. Davies, ed., "General Earl Cornwallis to General William Phillips, April 24, 1781," *Documents of the American Revolution*, vol. 20, 119.

5. Ibid.

6. Boyd, ed., "Lindsay Opie and James Ball to Governor Jefferson, April 12, 1781," *The Papers of Thomas Jefferson*, vol. 5, 424; Palmer, ed., "Capt. W. Thomas to Thomas Symonds, March 20, 1781," *Calendar of State Papers*, vol. 1, 583.

7. Palmer, ed., "Capt. W. Thomas to Thomas Symonds, March 20, 1781," *Calendar of State Papers*, vol. 1, 583.

8. Boyd, ed., "Henry Lee Sr. to Governor Jefferson, April 9, 1781," *The Papers of Thomas Jefferson*, vol. 5, 393–94.

9. Boyd, ed., "Peter Wagner to Governor Jefferson, April 3, 1781," *The Papers of Thomas Jefferson*, vol. 5, 335–36.

10. Boyd, ed., "Henry Lee Sr. to Governor Jefferson, April 9, 1781," *The Papers of Thomas Jefferson*, vol. 5, 393–94.

11. Ibid.

12. Ibid.

13. Ibid.

14. Boyd, ed., "John Skinker to Governor Jefferson, April 11, 1781," *The Papers of Thomas Jefferson*, vol. 5, 406.

15. Ibid.

16. Pleasants, ed., "Daniel Jenifer to Governor Thomas Sims Lee, April 8, 1781," *Maryland Archives*, vol. 47, 172–73.

17. Boyd, ed., "Edmund Read to Governor Jefferson, April 10, 1781," *The Papers of Thomas Jefferson*, vol. 5, 399.

18. Boyd, ed., "John Skinker to Governor Jefferson, April 11, 1781," *The Papers of Thomas Jefferson*, vol. 5, 406.

19. Boyd, ed., "Richard Henry Lee to Governor Jefferson, April 9, 1781," *The Papers of Thomas Jefferson*, vol. 5, 394.

20. Boyd, ed., "Edmund Read to Governor Jefferson, April 10, 1781," *The Papers of Thomas Jefferson*, vol. 5, 399.

21. Boyd, ed., "John Skinker to Governor Jefferson, April 11, 1781," *The Papers of Thomas Jefferson*, vol. 5, 406.

22. Boyd, ed., "Robert Mitchell to Governor Jefferson, April 12, 1781," *The Papers of Thomas Jefferson*, vol. 5, 423.

23. Ibid.

24. Ibid.

25. Pleasants, ed., "Joshua Beall to Governor Thomas Sim Lee," April 15, *Maryland Archives*, vol. 47, 188.

26. Idzerda, ed., "General Lafayette to General Washington, April 23,1781," *Lafayette in the Age of the American Revolution*, vol. 4, 60–61.

27. Ibid.

28. John C. Fitzgerald, ed., "George Washington to Lund Washington, April 30, 1781," *The Writings of George Washington*, vol. 22 (Washington, DC: US Government Printing Office, 1931), 14–15.

29. Marquis de Chastellux, *Travels in North America in the Years 1780, 1781, and 1782*, vol. 2, 597.

30. Ibid.

31. Ibid.

32. Ibid.

33. Ibid.

34. Pleasants, ed., "Joshua Beall to Governor Thomas Sims Lee, April 15, 1781," *Maryland Archives*, vol. 47, 188.

35. Willcox, ed., *The American Rebellion: Sir Henry Clinton's Narrative*, 280. Thomas Jefferson claimed General Phillips had 2,300 troops with him, and many secondary sources put the number at 2,500.

36. Simcoe, *Simcoe's Military Journal*, 189; Richard K. Macmaster, "The Journal of Dr. Robert Honeyman," *Virginia Magazine of History and Biography* 79, no. 4 (October 1971), 392; David John Mays, ed., "Edmund Pendleton to James Madison, April 30, 1781," *The Letters and Papers of Edmund Pendleton*, vol. 1 (Charlottesville: University Press of Virginia, 1967), 352.

37. Davies, ed., "General Arnold to General Clinton, May 12, 1781," *Documents of the American Revolution*, vol. 20, 142. A typical British light-infantry battalion was smaller than a regiment and was comprised of several light-infantry companies drawn from the regular regiments.

38. Boyd, ed., "To the County Lieutenants of Henrico and Certain Other Counties, April 19, 1781," *The Papers of Thomas Jefferson*, vol. 5, 496.

39. Simcoe, *Simcoe's Military Journal*, 190.

40. Ibid., 191.

41. Boyd, ed., "James Innes to Governor Jefferson, April 20, 1781," *The Papers of Thomas Jefferson*, vol. 5, 506.

42. Ibid.

43. Ibid.

44. Simcoe, *Simcoe's Military Journal*, 191.

45. Boyd, ed., "James Innes to Governor Jefferson, April 23, 1781," *The Papers of Thomas Jefferson*, vol. 5, 539–40.

46. Dennis Conrad, ed., "Steuben to Greene, April 25, 1781," *The Papers of General Nathanael Greene*, vol. 8 (Chapel Hill: University of North Carolina Press, 1995), 147.

47. Robert Davis, *The Revolutionary War: The Battle of Petersburg* (E. and R. Davis, 2002), 10.

48. Ibid.

49. Charles Campbell, ed., "Banister to Bland, May 16, 1781," *Bland Papers*, vol. 1 (Petersburg, VA: 1840), 68.

50. Davis, *The Revolutionary War: The Battle of Petersburg*, 12.

51. Ibid., 14.

52. Ibid., 16, 18.

53. Lillie DuPuy VanCulin Harper, ed., *Colonial Men and Times: Containing the Journal of Col. Daniel Trabue*, 90–91.

54. Davis, *The Revolutionary War: The Battle of Petersburg*, 20.

55. Lillie DuPuy VanCulin Harper, ed., *Colonial Men and Times: Containing the Journal of Col. Daniel Trabue*, 90–91.

56. Ibid., 90.

57. Conrad, ed., "Baron Steuben to General Greene, April 25, 1781," *The Papers of General Nathanael Greene*, vol. 8, 148.

58. Idzerda, ed., "General Lafayette to General Greene, April 28, 1781," *Lafayette in the Age of the American Revolution*, vol. 4, 68.

59. Muhlenberg, *The Life of Major-General Peter Muhlenberg*, 250.

60. Boyd, ed., "Thomas Jefferson to General Washington, May 9, 1781," *The Papers of Thomas Jefferson*, vol. 5, 623.

61. Tarleton, "General Benedict Arnold to General Henry Clinton, May 12, 1781," *A History of the Campaigns of 1780 and 1781 in the Southern Provinces of North America*, 335.

62. Conrad, ed., "Baron Steuben to General Greene, April 25, 1781," *The Papers of General Nathanael Greene*, vol. 8, 148.

63. Muhlenberg, *The Life of Major-General Peter Muhlenberg*, 250.

64. Conrad, ed., "Steuben to Greene, April 25, 1781," *The Papers of General Nathanael Greene*, vol. 8, 148.

65. Tarleton, "General Arnold to General Clinton, May 12, 1781," *A History of the Campaigns of 1780 and 1781 in the Southern Provinces of North America*, 335.

66. Ibid.

67. Ibid.

68. Boyd, ed., "James Maxwell to Thomas Jefferson, April 26, 1781," *The Papers of Thomas Jefferson*, vol. 5, 557.

69. Ibid., 558.

70. Ibid., 557.

71. Hugh Rankin, *The War of the Revolution in Virginia* (Williamsburg: Virginia Independence Bicentennial Commission, 1979), 31.

72. Simcoe, *Simcoe's Military Journal*, 199.

73. Simcoe, *Simcoe's Military Journal*, 200.

74. Rankin, *The War of the Revolution in Virginia*, 31–32.

75. Idzerda, ed., "General Lafayette to General Weedon, May 3, 1781," *Lafayette in the Age of the American Revolution*, vol. 4, 77.

76. Idzerda, ed., "General Lafayette to General Washington, May 4, 1781," *Lafayette in the Age of the American Revolution*, vol. 4, 82.

CHAPTER SIX: CORNWALLIS COMES TO VIRGINIA

1. Tarleton, *A History of the Campaigns of 1780 and 1781 in the Southern Provinces of North America*, 285–86.

2. Ibid., 285.

3. Idzerda, ed., "General Lafayette to General Greene, May 3, 1781," *Lafayette in the Age of the American Revolution*, vol. 4, 79.

4. Idzerda, ed., "General Lafayette to General Washington, May 4, 1781," *Lafayette in the Age of the American Revolution*, vol. 4, 83.

5. Ibid.

6. Idzerda, ed., "General Lafayette to the Chevalier de La Luzerne, May 3, 1781," *Lafayette in the Age of the American Revolution*, vol. 4, 89.

7. Idzerda, ed., "General Lafayette to General Weedon, May 15, 1781," *Lafayette in the Age of the American Revolution*, vol. 4, 104.

8. Idzerda, ed., "General Lafayette to General Greene, May 18, 1781," *Lafayette in the Age of the American Revolution*, vol. 4, 113.

9. John Selby, *The Revolution in Virginia: 1775–1783* (Colonial Williamsburg Foundation, 1988), 275.

10. Tarleton, 294.

11. Idzerda, ed., "General Lafayette to the Chevalier de La Luzerne, May 22, 1781," *Lafayette in the Age of the American Revolution*, vol. 4, 120.

12. Tarleton, "Earl Cornwallis to Sir Henry Clinton, May 26, 1781," *A History of the Campaigns of 1780 and 1781 in the Southern Provinces of North America*, 343.

13. Idzerda, ed., "General Lafayette to Governor Jefferson, May 28, 1781," *Lafayette in the Age of the American Revolution*, vol. 4, 136.

14. Ibid., 136–137.

15. Idzerda, ed., "General Lafayette to Governor Jefferson, May 31, 1781," *Lafayette in the Age of the American Revolution*, vol. 4, 149.

16. Idzerda, ed., "General Lafayette to General Weedon, June 1, 1781," *Lafayette in the Age of the American Revolution*, vol. 4, 158.

17. Tarleton, *A History of the Campaigns of 1780 and 1781 in the Southern Provinces of North America*, 295.

18. Tarleton, "Earl Cornwallis to Sir Henry Clinton, June 30, 1781," *A History of the Campaigns of 1780 and 1781 in the Southern Provinces of North America*, 348–49.

19. Tarleton, *A History of the Campaigns of 1780 and 1781 in the Southern Provinces of North America*, 295–96.

20. Ibid., 296.

21. Kranish, *Flight from Monticello*, 278.

22. Ibid., 279.

23. "Joseph Jones to George Washington, June 20, 1781," *Letters of Joseph Jones of Virginia, 1777–1787* (Washington, DC: Department of State, 1889), 82.

24. *Journal of the House of Delegates*, June 4, 1781 (Richmond: 1828), 10.

25. Jones, "Benjamin Harrison to Joseph Jones," *Letters of Joseph Jones of VA: 1777–87* (Washington, DC: Dept. of State, 1889), 82.

26. Ibid.

27. Tarleton, *A History of the Campaigns of 1780 and 1781 in the Southern Provinces of North America*, 296.

28. Ibid., 297.

29. Kranish, *Flight from Monticello*, 283.

30. Ibid., 284.

31. Tarleton, *A History of the Campaigns of 1780 and 1781 in the Southern Provinces of North America*, 297.

32. Ibid.

33. Ibid.

34. Simcoe, *Simcoe's Military Journal*, 212.

35. Ibid.

36. Idzerda, ed., "General Steuben to General Lafayette, June 3 and 5, 1781," *Lafayette in the Age of the American Revolution*, vol. 4, 166, 170.

37. Idzerda, ed., "General Steuben to General Lafayette, June 5, 1781," *Lafayette in the Age of the American Revolution*, vol. 4, 170.

38. Simcoe, *Simcoe's Military Journal*, 216.

39. Ibid., 217.

40. Ibid., 217–18.

41. Friedrich Kapp, *The Life of Frederick William von Steuben* (1859; New York: Corner House Historical Publications, 1999), 442.

42. Simcoe, *Simcoe's Military Journal*, 219.

43. Ibid., 220.

44. Ibid.
45. Ibid.
46. Kranish, *Flight from Monticello*, 292.
47. Idzerda, ed., "General Lafayette to General Steuben, June 13, 1781," *Lafayette in the Age of the American Revolution*, vol. 4, 179.
48. Idzerda, ed., "General Lafayette to the Chevalier de La Luzerne, June 16, 1781," *Lafayette in the Age of the American Revolution*, vol. 4, 186.
49. Ibid.
50. Idzerda, ed., "General Lafayette to the Chevalier de La Luzerne, June 16, 1781," and "General Lafayette to General Washington, June 18, 1781," *Lafayette in the Age of the American Revolution*, vol. 4, 186, 195.

CHAPTER SEVEN: SPENCER'S ORDINARY AND GREEN SPRING

1. Simcoe, *Simcoe's Military Journal*, 225.
2. Ewald, *Diary of the American War: A Hessian Journal*, 308.
3. Simcoe, *Simcoe's Military Journal*, 228.
4. Ibid.
5. Ibid.
6. Ibid.
7. Ibid.
8. Ewald, *Diary of the American War: A Hessian Journal*, 309.
9. Ibid. Ewald's reference to the Wild Irish Riflemen is difficult to ascertain, but it is likely a reference to the Virginia frontier riflemen, many of Scotch-Irish and German descent, who had joined Lafayette's army.
10. Simcoe, *Simcoe's Military Journal*, 32.
11. Ewald, *Diary of the American War: A Hessian Journal*, 309.
12. Ibid.
13. Idzerda, ed., *Lafayette in the Age of the American Revolution*, vol. 4, 217n2.
14. Idzerda, ed., "General Lafayette to Thomas Nelson, June 28, 1781," *Lafayette in the Age of the American Revolution*, vol. 4, 217–18.
15. Tarleton, "General Cornwallis to General Clinton, June 30, 1781," *A History of the Campaigns of 1780 and 1781 in the Southern Provinces of North America*, 350.
16. Simcoe, *Simcoe's Military Journal*, 234.
17. Ewald, *Diary of the American War: A Hessian Journal*, 312.
18. Davies, ed. "General Clinton to General Cornwallis, June 11, 1781," 157–58.
19. Davies, ed., "General Cornwallis to General Clinton, June 30, 1781," 166.
20. Ibid.
21. Jared Sparks, ed., "General Wayne to General Washington, July 8, 1781," *Correspondence of the American Revolution Being Letters of Eminent Men to George Washington* (Boston: Little, Brown, 1853), 348.
22. Tarleton, "Earl Cornwallis to Sir Henry Clinton, July 8, 1781," *A History of the Campaigns of 1780 and 1781 in the Southern Provinces of North America*, 400.

23. *Caledonian Mercury*, October 10, 1781, "Extract of a letter from an officer in the 76th Regiment dated on board the Lord Mulgrave transport, Hampton Road, Virginia, July 23, 1781," 3.

24. Gillard Hunt, ed., "Colonel John Francis Mercer," *Eyewitness Account of the American Revolution: Fragments of Revolutionary History* (Rpt. in *The New York Times* and Arno Press, 1971), 48.

25. Ibid., 47–48.

26. Ibid., 48.

27. Ibid., 49.

28. "Major William Galvan to Richard Peters, July 8, 1781," *Gazette of the American Friends of Lafayette* 1, no. 1 (February 1942), 3.

29. Ibid., 3.

30. Ibid.

31. Ibid.

32. Sparks, ed., "General Wayne to General Washington, July 8, 1781," *Correspondence of the American Revolution Being Letters of Eminent Men to George Washington*, 348.

33. Peter Decher, ed., *Journal of Lt. William Feltman of the First Pennsylvania Regiment, 1781–1782* (Samen, NH: Ayer Co., 1969), 7.

34. Ebenezer Denny, *Military Journal of Major Ebenezer Denny* (Philadelphia: J. B. Lippincott and Co., 1859), 37.

35. Ibid.

36. Tarleton, *A History of the Campaigns of 1780 and 1781 in the Southern Provinces of North America*, 354.

37. "Major William Galvan to Richard Peters, July 8, 1781," *Gazette of the American Friends of Lafayette* 1, no. 1 (February 1942), 4.

38. Ibid.

39. Sparks, ed., "General Wayne to General Washington, July 8, 1781," *Correspondence of the American Revolution Being Letters of Eminent Men to George Washington*, 348.

40. *Pennsylvania Packet*, July 21, 1781, "Extract of a letter from an officer of rank, July 11, 1781."

41. Ibid.

42. Henry P. Johnson, *The Yorktown Campaign and the Surrender of Cornwallis: 1781* (1881; Ft. Washington, PA: Eastern National, 1997), 190.

43. Tarleton, "General Cornwallis to Tarleton, July 8, 1781," *A History of the Campaigns of 1780 and 1781 in the Southern Provinces of North America*, 402.

44. Ibid.

45. Ibid., 402–03.

46. Idzerda, ed., "General Lafayette to General Washington, July 20, 1781," *Lafayette in the Age of the American Revolution*, vol. 4, 256.

47. Tarleton, *A History of the Campaigns of 1780 and 1781 in the Southern Provinces of North America*, 358.

48. Idzerda, ed., "General Lafayette to General Washington, July 20, 1781," *Lafayette in the Age of the American Revolution*, vol. 4, 256.

49. Tarleton, "General Clinton to General Cornwallis, July 15, 1781," *A History of the Campaigns of 1780 and 1781 in the Southern Provinces of North America*, 404–5.

50. Tarleton, "General Clinton to General Cornwallis, July 11, 1781," *A History of the Campaigns of 1780 and 1781 in the Southern Provinces of North America*, 404.

BIBLIOGRAPHY

PRIMARY SOURCES

Boyd, Julian P., ed. *The Papers of Thomas Jefferson*. Vols. 3–6. Princeton, NJ: Princeton University Press, 1950–51.

Campbell, Charles, ed. *The Bland Papers: Being a Selection from a Manuscript of Colonel Theodorick Bland Jr. of Prince George County, Virginia*. Vol. 1. Petersburg: Edmund and Julian Ruffin, 1840.

Commager, Henry Steele. *Documents of American History*. New York: Appleton-Century-Crofts, 1963.

Commager, Henry Steele, and Richard B. Morris, eds. *The Spirit of Seventy-Six*. Edison, NJ: Castle Books, 2002.

Conrad, Dennis, ed. *The Papers of General Nathanael Greene*. Vol. 8. Chapel Hill: University of North Carolina Press, 1995.

Davies, K. G., ed. *Documents of the American Revolution*. The Colonial Series. Vols. 18–20. Shannon: Irish University Press, 1976–79.

De Chastellux, Marquis. *Travels in North America in the Years 1780, 1781, and 1782*. Vol. 2. *The New York Times* and Arno Press, 1968.

Decher, Peter, ed. *Journal of Lt. William Feltman of the First Pennsylvania Regiment, 1781–1782*. Samen, NH: Ayer Co., 1969.

Denny, Ebenezer. *Military Journal of Major Ebenezer Denny*. Philadelphia: J. B. Lippincott and Co., 1859.

Dorman, John, ed. *Virginia Revolutionary Pension Applications*. Vol. 12. Washington, DC: 1965.

Ewald, Captain Johann. *Diary of the American War: A Hessian Journal*. Edited and translated by Joseph Tustin. New Haven: Yale University Press, 1979.

Fitzpatrick, John C. *The Writings of George Washington from the Original Manuscripts, 1745–1799*. Washington, DC: US Government Printing Office, 1931.

Force, Peter, ed. *American Archives: 5th Series*. Vols. 1–3. Washington, DC: US Congress, 1848–1853.

Ford, Worthington C., et al., eds. *Journals of the Continental Congress*. Vols. 1–27. Washington, DC: US Government Printing Office, 1904–37.

Graham, Major William. *General Joseph Graham and His Papers on North Carolina Revolutionary History*. Raleigh, NC: Edwards and Broughton, 1904.

Hamilton, Stanislaus M., ed. *Letters to Washington and Accompanying Papers.* Vol. 5. Boston: Houghton Mifflin Co., 1902.

Harper, Lillie DuPuy VanCulin, ed. *Colonial Men and Times: Containing the Journal of Col. Daniel Trabue.* Philadelphia: Innes and Sons, 1916.

Hunt, Gillard, ed. *Eyewitness Accounts of the American Revolution: Fragments of Revolutionary History.* Reprinted by *The New York Times* and Arno Press, 1971.

Idzerda, Stanley J., ed. *Lafayette in the Age of the American Revolution: Selected Letters and Papers.* Vols. 1–3. Ithaca, NY: Cornell University Press, 1980.

Jones, Alfred E., ed. *The Journal of Alexander Chesney, a South Carolina Loyalist in the Revolution and After.* Printed from a copy belonging to the Ohio State Library, 1921.

Jones, Joseph. *Letters of Joseph Jones of VA: 1777–87.* Washington, DC: Dept. of State, 1889.

Journal of Continental Congress. Accessed via the Library of Congress website at www.loc.gov.

Journal of the House of Delegates. Richmond, VA: State Library, 1828.

Lamb, Roger. *An Original and Authentic Journal of Occurrences During the Late American War.* Dublin: Wilkinson and Courtney, 1809.

Laughton, John K., ed. *The Journal of Rear-Admiral Bartholomew James.* London: Navy Records Society, 1896.

Lengel, Edward, ed. *The Papers of George Washington.* Vol. 20. Charlottesville: University Press of Virginia, 2010.

Martin, Joseph Plum. *Private Yankee Doodle.* Eastern Acorn Press, 1962.

McIlwaine, H. R., ed. *Journals of the Council of the State of Virginia.* Vol. 1. Richmond, 1931.

Moore, Frank. *Diary of the American Revolution, from Newspapers and Original Documents.* 2 vols. New York: Charles Scribner, 1860. Reprinted in *The New York Times* and Arno Press, 1969.

Palmer, William, ed. *Calendar of Virginia State Papers.* Vol. 1. 1875.

Pleasants, J. Hall, ed. *Maryland Archives.* Vol. 47. Maryland Historical Society, 1930.

Powell, Robert. *Biographical Sketch of Col. Levin Powell, 1737–1810: Including his Correspondence during the Revolutionary War.* Alexandria, VA: G. H. Ramey and Son, 1877.

Rice, Howard C., and Anne S. K. Brown, eds. and trans. *The American Campaigns of Rochambeau's Army: 1780–1783.* Vols. 1–2. Princeton, NJ: Princeton University Press, 1972.

Roberts, John M., ed. *Autobiography of a Revolutionary Soldier.* New York: Arno Press, 1979.

Ryan, Dennis P. *A Salute to Courage: The American Revolution as Seen Through Wartime Writings of Officers of the Continental Army and Navy.* New York: Columbia University Press, 1979.

Saffell, W. T. R. *Records of the Revolutionary War*, third edition. Baltimore: Charles Saffell, 1894.

Scheer, George, and Hugh Rankin, eds. *Rebels and Redcoats: The American Revolution Through the Eyes of Those Who Fought and Lived It.* New York: Da Capo Press, 1957.

Scribner, Robert L., and Brent Tarter, eds. *Revolutionary Virginia: The Road to Independence.* Vols. 1–7. Charlottesville: University Press of Virginia, 1973–1978.

Showman, Richard K. *The Papers of General Nathanael Greene.* Vol. 7. Chapel Hill: University of North Carolina Press, 1994.

Simcoe, Lt. Col. John. *Simcoe's Military Journal: A History of the Operations of a Partisan Corps Called the Queen's Rangers, Commanded by Lieut. Col. J. G. Simcoe, During the War of Revolution.* New York: *The New York Times* and Arno Press, 1968.

Smith, Paul H., ed. *Letters of Delegates to Congress: 1774–1789.* Washington, DC: Library of Congress, 1976.

Sparks, Jared, ed. *Correspondence of the American Revolution Being Letters of Eminent Men to George Washington.* Boston: Little, Brown, 1853.

Tarleton, Banastre. *A History of the Campaigns of 1780 and 1781 in the Southern Provinces of North America.* 1787; North Stratford, NH: Ayer Co., 1999.

Thacher, James. *A Military Journal during the American Revolutionary War.* Hartford, CT: S. Andrus and Son, 1854. Reprinted in New York: Arno Press, 1969.

Uhlendorf, Bernard, ed. and trans. *The Siege of Charleston with an Account of the Province of South Carolina: Diaries and Letters of Hessian Officers from the von Jungkenn Papers in the William L. Clements Library.* Vol. 12. Ann Arbor: University of Michigan Press, 1938.

Willcox, William B., ed. *The American Rebellion: Sir Henry Clinton's Narrative of His Campaigns, 1775–1782.* New Haven: Yale University Press, 1954.

SECONDARY SOURCES

Babits, Lawrence E. *A Devil of a Whipping: The Battle of Cowpens.* Chapel Hill: University of North Carolina Press, 1998.

Babits, Lawrence E., and Joshua B. Howard. *Long, Obstinate, and Bloody: The Battle of Guilford Courthouse.* Chapel Hill: University of North Carolina Press, 2009.

Baker, Thomas. *Another Such Victory: The Story of the American Defeat at Guilford Courthouse That Helped Win the War for Independence.* Ft. Washington, PA: Eastern National, 2005.

Boatner III, Mark M. *Encyclopedia of the American Revolution.* Mechanicsburg, PA: Stackpole Books, 1966.

Buchanan, John. *The Road to Guilford Courthouse: The American Revolution in the Carolinas.* New York: John Wiley and Sons, 1997.

Cecere, Michael. *Great Things Are Expected from the Virginians: Virginia in the American Revolution.* Westminster, MD: Heritage Books, 2008.

Cecere, Michael. *Wedded to My Sword: The Revolutionary War Service of Light Horse Harry Lee.* Westminster, MD: Heritage Books, 2012.

Davis, Robert. *The Revolutionary War: The Battle of Petersburg.* E. and R. Davis, 2002.

Draper, Lyman C. *King's Mountain and Its Heroes: History of the Battle of King's Mountain.* Cincinnati: Peter G. Thomson, 1881.

Friar, Robert. *The Militia are Coming in from all Quarters: The Revolution in Virginia's Lower Counties.* 2010.

Grainger, John D. *The Battle of Yorktown, 1781: A Reassessment.* Woodbridge, Suffolk: Boydell Press, 2005.

Greene, Jerome A. *The Guns of Independence: The Siege of Yorktown, 1781.* El Dorado Hills, CA: Savas Beatie, 2005.

Johnson, Henry P. *The Yorktown Campaign and the Surrender of Cornwallis: 1781.* 1881; Ft. Washington, PA: Eastern National, 1997.

Kapp, Friedrich. *The Life of Frederick William von Steuben.* 1859; New York: Corner House Historical Publications, 1999.

Kranish, Michael. *Flight from Monticello: Thomas Jefferson at War.* Oxford: Oxford University Press, 2010.

Lee, Henry. *The Revolutionary War Memoirs of General Henry Lee.* 1812; New York: Da Capo Press, 1998.

Lee, Nell Moore. *Patriot Above Profit: A Portrait of Thomas Nelson Jr., Who Supported the American Revolution with His Purse and Sword.* Nashville, TN: Rutledge Hill Press, 1988.

Marshall, John. *The Life of George Washington.* Vol. 2. Fredericksburg, VA: Citizens Guild of Washington's Boyhood Home, 1926.

Muhlenberg, Henry A. *The Life of Major-General Peter Muhlenberg.* Philadelphia: Cary and Hart, 1849.

O'Kelly, Patrick. *Nothing but Blood and Slaughter: The Revolutionary War in the Carolinas.* Vol. 2. Lillington, NC: Blue House Tavern Press, 2004.

Posey, John Thornton. *General Thomas Posey: Son of the American Revolution.* East Lansing: Michigan State University Press, 1992.

Rankin, Hugh F. *The War of the Revolution in Virginia*. Williamsburg: Virginia Independence Bicentennial Commission, 1979.

Selby, John. *The Revolution in Virginia: 1775–1783*. Colonial Williamsburg Foundation, 1988.

Stedman, C. *The History of the Origin, Progress, and Termination of the American War*. Vols. 1–2. London, 1794.

Stille, Charles. *Major-General Anthony Wayne and the Pennsylvania Line in the Continental Army*. 1893; Port Washington, NY: Kenniket Press, 1968.

Ward, Harry M. *Duty, Honor, or Country: General George Weedon and the American Revolution*. Philadelphia: American Philosophical Society 1979.

Williams, Mrs., ed. *Biography of Revolutionary Heroes*, 1839.

JOURNALS AND ARTICLES

Egle, Wm. H., ed. "Diary of Captain James Duncan of Colonel Moses Hazen's Regiment in the Yorktown Campaign, 1781." *Pennsylvania Archives*. Second Series. Vol. 15. 1890.

Elmer, Ebenezer. "The Journal of Ebenezer Elmer," *The Pennsylvania Magazine of History and Biography* 35. Philadelphia: Historical Society of Pennsylvania, 1911.

"Expedition to Portsmouth." *The William and Mary Quarterly* 12. Second Series, no. 3 (July 1932).

"Kings Mountain Expedition." *An Annual Publication of Historical Papers: Governor W. W. Holden and Revolutionary Documents*. Third Series. Durham, NC: Historical Society of Trinity College, 1899.

Macmaster, Richard K. "The Journal of Dr. Robert Honeyman." *Virginia Magazine of History and Biography* 79, no. 4 (October 1971).

"Major William Galvan to Richard Peters, July 8, 1781." *Gazette of the American Friends of Lafayette* 1, no. 1 (February 1942).

McMichael, James. "The Diary of Lt. James McMichael of the Pennsylvania Line, 1776–1778." *Pennsylvania Magazine of History and Biography* 16, no. 2 (1892).

"Narrative of the Duke de Lauzun." *Magazine of American History* 6 (1881).

Riley, Edward M., ed. "St. George Tucker's Journal of the Siege of Yorktown, 1781." *William and Mary Quarterly* 5, no. 3 (July 1948).

Seymour, William. "Journal of the Southern Expedition, 1780–1783." *The Pennsylvania Magazine of History and Biography* 7 (1883).

"Sir George Collier to General Sir Henry Clinton, May 16, 1779." *William and Mary Quarterly* 12. Second Series, no. 3 (July 1930).

NEWSPAPERS

Caledonian Mercury. October 10, 1781.

Connecticut Journal. February 15, 1781.

New York Gazette and Weekly Mercury. February 5, 1781.

New York Royal Gazette. February 3, 1781.

New York Royal Gazette. February 7, 1781.

Pennsylvania Gazette and Weekly Advertiser. October 31, 1781.

Pennsylvania Packet. July 21, 1781.

UNPUBLISHED SOURCES

"Embarkation Return for the Following Corps, December 11, 1780, New York." *Sir Henry Clinton Papers.* 113:15. University of Michigan, William L. Clements Library.

ACKNOWLEDGMENTS

I AM INDEBTED TO A NUMBER OF PEOPLE FOR THEIR HELP AND encouragement with this book. The folks at the *Journal of the American Revolution*—Todd Andrlik and particularly Don Hagist, who encouraged me to write the book and reviewed the manuscript, were instrumental in the completion of this work. Thanks are also due to Bruce H. Franklin of Westholme Publishing, who guided me through the publishing process, and copyeditor Alex Kane, who corrected my many mistakes. Fellow author Todd Braisted shared his immense knowledge of loyalist forces with me, while several of my friends and fellow reenactors in southeastern Virginia—most notably, Drummond Ball, Rob Friar, Buzz Deemer, Norm Fuss, and Jim Gallagher—offered their assistance in this project. I am grateful to all for their assistance and encouragement.

INDEX

lack of Tory support and, 81
letters from Clinton about French-
American offensive against
New York and, 135
letter to Lord George Germain
and, 92-93
meeting with Phillips at Petersburg and, 113-114
move to Portsmouth and, 145
occupying Richmond and, 129
Patrick Ferguson and, 3-4, 6-9, 40
poor condition of Greene's army
and, 40-41
protecting the king's friends and,
69
pursuit of the American light
corps and, 45-48, 51-55, 64-
65
resting army at Elk Hill Plantation
and, 126-127
shift in strategy and, 121
Virginia as key to Greene's army
and, 115
Williams effort to draw him away
from Morgan and, 49
Cornwallis, 18, 21
Cowans Ford, 46-47
Cowpens, battle of, xiii, 4, 42-43,
45, 47, 55, 75
Cross Creek, 73, 81
Cuckoo Tavern, 121
Culpeper County, 121
Cypress Creek, 37, 39

Dan River, 47-49, 51, 53-54, 64-66
Dauge's Bridge, 59
Davidson, William, 46-47
Declaration of Independence, 24
Delight, 8
Denny, Ebenezer, 142
DePeyser, Abraham, 7
Destouches, Chevalier, 90
Devil's Elbow Swamp, 58
Dick, John, 105
Dundas, Thomas, 13, 23, 36, 83,
86, 103, 106, 138

Eightieth Edinburgh Royal Volunteers Regiment, 13
Eightieth Regiment, 15, 17, 23, 27,
35-36, 83, 101, 106, 111,
137-138
Elizabeth River, 8, 55-57, 86
Elk Hill, 126-127
Elk Hill Plantation, 126
Ewald, Johann, 13, 16-17, 19, 22-
28, 31-32, 34-36, 38, 56-63,
86-90, 130-132, 134

Faden, William, 107
Faulkner, Ralph, 105-106
Feltman, William, 142
Ferguson, Patrick, 3-4, 6-9, 40
First Pennsylvania Regiment, 136,
142
Fluvanna River, 124, 126
Fort Frederick, 10
Fort Ticonderoga, 12
Forty-third Regiment, 138
Four Mile Creek, 24, 31
Fourth Virginia Regiment, 37
Fowey, 13, 87
Francisco, Peter, 80

Galvan, William, 136, 140-143
Georgetown, 2, 97
Germain, George, 46, 92-93
German jaegers, 9, 13, 67, 101
Germantown, battle of, 37
Gilbert Town, 3
Gillies, James, 49-50
Goode's Bridge, 144
Graham, Joseph, 68, 70
Graves, Thomas, 100
Great Bridge, battle of, xiii, 37, 56-
58, 62, 82-83, 86
Greene, Nathanael
arrival of long-awaited reinforce-
ments and, 73
battle of Guilford Courthouse
and, 73, 75-76, 81
battle of Petersburg and, 110-111
Cornwallis's pursuit of, 49, 51-55,
72-74